NEVERFAILS

30 DAYS ON **MARRIAGE**

BRIAN SUMNER

CONTENTS

ACKNOWLEDGMENTS

First and foremost, I would like to acknowledge my Lord and Savior, Jesus Christ, for the cross, the sacrifice, and the love. Thank You!

My wife, Tracy, who, for every time you have called me crazy, have been reminded that it is you who are actually the crazier one for marrying me twice.

My children—Dakota, Eden, and Jude—who encourage me daily as I see you learn and grow in the ways of our Lord.

To my parents, who supported my sisters and I, fought for them, and were married for forty-four years, holding to the covenant they once made.

To you the reader, who, as you partake of this book with an open heart and hands to receive, will find in these pages both God's Word and life's experiences. May they encourage and convict you, as you sow good things into your marriage.

I would also like to take this time to thank Romy Godding, Tom Donohue, and the many people who helped to make this book possible. Your encouragement in reading, editing, feedback, and more is eternally appreciated. And special thanks to Chad Vondra for his online support.

Finally, thanks to Whitney Schey at WhitneyDarling.com for the cover photo, Freshpark.com for the portrait, and James Noble for the book design.

God bless you all.

Brian Sumner

†

INTRODUCTION

Where to begin? What to say? What is the goal here? Well, as you may know, I have been married twice, both times to the same woman. No, I'm not mental, but as many can attest, as good as many things may be, when two selfish people come together without a proper understanding of marriage, only a few things need to go wrong to put your marriage into that downward spiral, which can ultimately end in divorce.

For me, a Liverpudlian by birth, making my way over to America to skateboard as a teen, I didn't know the first thing about marriage. Throw in the fact I had never been raised with any kind of faith, had given the latter years of my teens to professional skateboarding and its lifestyle, and then married a half-Italian, half-Mexican girl born and raised in Huntington Beach, California, who was also without faith.

So yeah, you end up with quite an interesting story.

We were together for four months, secretly married, had a child, began to fight, divorced, came to faith, remarried, and went on to have two more children. I'm thirty-five today, and we have been together for over fifteen years.

Though I have thought about writing a book for some years, it was after I came to faith in 2004 and began sharing our story that I was exposed to just how much pain and hurt there is both in Christian and non-Christian marriages. I knew this project needed to happen.

I'm not an English major, nor am I looking to be an author or hoping to hit the jackpot. I just realized my wife and I had "lived the book" on how *not* to be married. Then, once we became believers, by way of survival and witness and as God was restoring our marriage, I knew it was time to write a book on how to be married.

As a skateboarder, you spend long hours perfecting tricks and filming with photographers and cinematographers. Everything has to be perfect, just right, no hands touching the ground, and with the tricks having lots of style. With this mindset, would I ever be able to write or finish a book? Could I release something that simply revealed our mess of a marriage, yet showed the beauty within? It seemed like a struggle.

It was when a couple (who are now good friends) sent me a message one day that I knew it was time to start writing.

They had read many of the social media posts I had been putting out, and many topics had spoken to them. This day was different. An affair had taken place in the marriage, and they requested we meet up for coffee right away.

Hopping into my car and arriving at the local Starbucks, I was met by a man who appeared emotionally drained, paranoid, and neurotic. His wife sat slouched in her chair, Jackie O glasses covering her eyes. Both of them were unable to talk.

Finally, as they addressed how they both felt, gathering together whatever sentences they could, to their shock, I began to chuckle. I began to laugh to myself as I thought about this situation. Here before me was an opportunity to see a couple fight and give their all to God; and it was this that brought such joy. You see, he wanted to forgive and move on, believe for the best, and honor God in this covenant he had made. And the wife, even though she had fallen, was a mess, and felt unworthy, she was repentant and eager to bring glory both to her God and her husband.

As these thoughts meandered through my mind, I felt the peace of God. It was evident that God was about to be lifted up and that He was still eager to pastor this marriage.

After we talked and prayed and they left to visit with family for support, on the drive home a thought would not leave my mind. As much Scripture as I had shared, as much prayer and direction, what if I had a book about the very things I have lived and experienced? A book not to replace the Bible, but to highlight God's Word and what it has done to rebuild my own marriage. A book that would show what God Himself has done in my own home, both to bring me to die to self more and to learn to love my bride like Christ loves His bride, the church.

My wife and I have spent many an evening in times of prayer and devotion, both blessed and tough seasons. Spending those moments together every night built in us an appetite for meeting together before the Lord for strength and encouragement.

The thought that if only I had something for this couple to read for the next thirty days, something that would bond them together, openly addressing where they may be in life, couldn't I possibly help them even more? Were our struggles in marriage for nothing, or did God intend us to use this part of our testimony to point to God's goodness?

These and other thoughts led to the writing of this book. The goal is not to give you something to religiously clock in to for fifteen minutes, then go on to watch two hours of whatever is on the local brainwash box. It is meant to challenge you to give time and effort to your marriage, a book that should cause you to sacrifice your time in the hopes of implementing these principles into your life.

You see, I was depressed, over living, and divorced at one time, but Jesus Christ saved both my wife and me. He restored our lives and is still at work in us today.

Because of this, I offer a warning: the goal of this book is for you to grab a hold of the deep biblical truths of God's Word, with the hopes of your marriage becoming an even greater light and pointing others to Jesus. I was going to call this book "death by marriage," as, after all, we are to "die daily," "carry our cross," and become more Christlike. But that title was taken, so instead, the title is based around the one thing that "Never Fails"—LOVE!

The book is broken down into three main sections. The first ten chapters focus on doctrine: understanding God's plan and purpose for our lives. The next ten chapters dig in to the practical ways we are together, as one, directed by God's Word. And finally, the last ten chapters center on the more personal ways you and your spouse interact based on the current issues I have experienced or seen in marriages at this time.

Many Christians, including myself, say we are following Christ while choosing things contrary to His clear guidance for our marriages. So my challenge to you today is this: do you want a nice little pat-you-on-the-back book? Or do you want a book that will help you in the struggle that is marriage? We need to turn down the other voices in order to hear God's voice clearly.

I was sitting in my friend's shop one day, and while we were conversing, he stopped me and told me he needed to pray. In his prayers for my wife and me, he began to tell us we were called to marriage ministry and that the struggles we had faced in our own marriage he saw as the bricks of a bridge—that as we opened up about them, they would help strengthen the bonds and structures of the marriages around us. Thanks Chris.

For Tracy and me, it was crystal clear. Only that morning I had prayed and sought the Lord on marriage ministry specifically. That week we were bombarded by phone calls from many of our good friends who began to reach out to us to speak into their marriages.

I hope and pray that today, as you begin reading about the ups and downs in our walks, that God will be all the more lifted up and the bonds of trust and unity will begin to be restored as your marriages are strengthened.

As you get into this, remember, "Love never fails."

DAY 1: LOVE NEVER FAILS!

Pulling up to a chapel … right off the Vegas strip … my wife-to-be and I were sure our love would last. Though we had no faith and knew almost nothing about the Bible, we both walked down the aisle, crying as the pastor read:

> Love is patient, love is kind. It does not envy, it does not boast, it is not proud. It does not dishonor others, it is not self-seeking, it is not easily angered, it keeps no record of wrongs. Love does not delight in evil but rejoices with the truth. It always protects, always trusts, always hopes, always perseveres. Love never fails.
>
> *1 Corinthians 13:4–8*

"Love never fails." Never fails? Sounds amazing! We'll take it!

And so we said "I DO" and drove off into the night.

As mentioned in the introduction, the next few years found us heading into divorce, and then through faith in Christ, getting remarried. Through this process, we learned a lot about what true love is.

One of the things you should know for sure is that the truth sets you free (John 8:32). So I'll just step out and say it (after all we are going to be spending the next thirty days together). So here goes: You've been fooled, hijacked, lied to, led astray, ripped off, and if you like, DECEIVED. Face it, you have and you know it. We all know it but maybe we just haven't admitted it yet. We are born into a world where things are already in motion, where there are already mindsets that every last one of us falls prey to. As I travel the world giving my testimony, I share how in the beginning, my wife and I first fell in love, how we loved the way each other looked, the way we made one another feel, the way we treated each other. So why did our marriage fail? Why did we fight, get jealous, become bitter, fight some more, and end up divorced? Did our love fail?

If you go back and think about the emotions you felt when you first met that "special someone," if you are being perfectly honest, the person you were really in love with is yourself. You might have felt eager, romantic, passionate, obsessed. You might have even said that you "would die for them," but truthfully speaking, did you really love that person?

The world describes love as passion, romance, lust, and everything *felt*. It's a twisted notion of love hidden behind a veil. We live in a world where we throw the word love around so casually that it has lost its meaning. Do we actually know the true, biblical definition of love? (And by this, I mean God's love! He knows best, after all.)

Test yourself. Do you really *love* chocolate, coffee, your pet hamster, your spouse, your favorite show, that one band, your kids, and God with the same amount of love? You don't have to answer. I'm sure you get the point. So what does it really mean to love?

While we have one word for love in our English language, other languages, like Greek and Hebrew, have many. And it's in the Greek that *agape*, the most famous word for biblical love, is used. Agape is used in the 1 Corinthians 13 passage, and it speaks of a spiritual and sacrificial love. This kind of love gives whether it gets love in return or not. The best way to describe it is how Christians have used it since New Testament times, in pointing to God's unconditional love for us. And what better love is there than God's unconditional love?

> But God demonstrates his own love (agape) for us in this: While we were still sinners, Christ died for us.
>
> *Romans 5:8*

Amazing. Jesus Himself said, "Love one another. As I have loved you ..." (John 13:34). He began that passage with "A new *command* I give you: Love one another." A command, not a suggestion.

I think to myself, did I love my Tracy this way? Was it unconditional, or conditional—as long as she kept *my* conditions? In truth, I was willing to give my all as long as there was something in it for me. If there wasn't, it was back to loving myself. This, thankfully, began to change, and it needs to change for you too. You see, agape is a love that chooses to give and chooses to die to self for the sake of the other person. You will only feel like a doormat if you are doing all of this for yourself, putting conditions on your love. But if you love unconditionally, sacrificially, with agape, you will be choosing to love your spouse for their sake and not your own.

It's here that you have to stop and ask, where are you in your marriage? Where are you as a couple? Has your willingness to pursue one another out of selfish desires been revealed in your hearts? Have you missed the true love that you thought you were giving? I can tell you today, God chose to put His love on me, He chose to accept me where I was, with all of my shortcomings, and He chose to go to the cross *for me*. No different for you. So here, today and now, because "love never fails," can you choose, as God did in Christ, to give your unconditional love to your spouse, overlooking their shortcomings and idio-syncrasies? Have faith and hope and extend mercy and grace along the journey, believing that you will tap into the agape love that your relationship was meant to be wrapped in. After all, "God is love!" (1 John 4:8).

Friends, I want to encourage you, this path before us shouldn't be viewed as a burden, but a blessing. If your relationship is upside down, understand where you are and learn from where you have been; things can only get better.

Today! First Corinthians 13:8: Love never fails.

For me, it's very easy to sit back and think, "Wow, God, You restored our marriage! We are no longer divorced but together, 'one' again." But just because we're not divorced doesn't mean we won't have hard times or face new challenges. We have to walk in God's love every day. I remember years ago, coming to understand more of how God loves me and thinking to myself, *I can't love my wife like that! I can't love as deeply and as on purpose as God does.* That day was very liberating for me. If I try to love her in my own power, my own strength, white-knuckling it, I will be relying on my ways, my abilities—myself. What we need to learn to do with our spouses is to love them as Jesus loves us. But how did He do that? He trusted in the Father daily and walked in the Holy Spirit.

So I encourage you to trust the Lord and give Him control of your rela-tionship with your spouse. Allow the Lord to guide you on this journey to better understand and know what His love is like. This also takes the pressure off you, and you won't have to try to complete this thirty-day journey in your own strength, but in His. Love your partner as a child of God first, then as your spouse.

As we begin this first day of thirty, let's let go of everything, overlook the things our worldly love has caused us to believe, and choose instead to agape love our spouses, as our heavenly Father chose to agape love us.

His love never fails.

DAY 2: ARE WE HIS SHEEP?

God chose to love us when we were unlovable and has called us to love our spouses unconditionally. Therefore, it would do us good to get a grasp, right here and now, of what we actually believe and figure out why we are reading this book.

Because of our testimony, my wife and I are always in conversation or some kind of contact with people about their relationships. Oftentimes they relate to our story, having been through a divorce and remarriage, or they are facing hard times and looking for some advice or guidance. I'm often amazed at how many couples or spouses have reached out to us, looking for help with their relationships. They start by sharing their list of "justifications" for how they came to be Christians. Things like how they were raised in the church, their dad is a pastor, their grandparents are praying for them, they are currently playing in the worship band, or even serving in some other kind of ministry. Yet, these same people seem to hold fast to every bit of advice from all types of people and either choose to ignore or are ignorant of what God's Word says or what God may be saying to them.

We have to quit playing church and let go of our justifications or any ignorance. God's Word tells us plainly, "What God has joined together, let not man seperate" (Mark 10:9, NKJV). Our call is to "follow" Jesus, which means heeding His Word. Do we hear His voice? We are born into this world as sinners, needing a new heart and being granted that new heart by what Jesus did on the cross, if we repent. He lived a perfect life, took our sins upon the cross, shed His blood to cover our sins and pay for them, died a sinner's death, and rose again on the third day. He alone is able to grant us eternal life and confirm our salvation and help us by the Holy Spirit. Thank You, Lord!

Did you get that? Are we on the same page? We need to be able to hear His words clearly. Let's see why this is so important.

In God's Word Jesus says, "My Sheep hear My Voice, and I know them, and they follow Me" (John 10:27, NKJV). Jesus said this and He meant it. He is the shepherd—you are His sheep. Do you hear His voice? Are you following after Him? Are you reading, learning, and applying His Word to your life today?

People like me, an author writing a book, or even a pastor helping and counseling you, are just "under-shepherds," vessels carrying His message to you. In all of the work and care we may provide, the most important thing is that you are hearing Jesus' voice. He is the one who daily opens the gate, yearning to spend time with you, examining your wounds, knowing the things you are experiencing, and guiding you away from the dangers that may be lurking around the corner.

All of this being said ... again, please, today, here and now, make sure you are not listening to or following Brian, your pastor, or some other person you have reached out to. Instead, make sure you are following the Lord as people like myself, pastors, friends, and family point you to Him; hear His voice.

I say this as both an encouragement and a warning. We are not Christians because we go to church, can quote Scripture, or know the songs. We are Christians because of the work Christ has done and is still doing in us today.

We can't take all the verses in the Bible we like about eternal life, His providing for us, but throw away all the verses where He calls us to be attentive, to do something, or to listen to our Shepherd (for our own safety, I might add).

Now, along with your partner, ask each other these three questions:

1. Do you believe Jesus is who He claimed to be and are you following Him?

2. Do you understand He speaks to us through Scripture, that He inspired it, and that He expects us to search His Word and follow it as He leads us in life?

3. Do you understand the reason He planned it this way is because He knows what is best for us, He has a plan for our marriage, and this means our stepping out of the way from playing "god," and trusting Him as our God?

It's only after you can answer "YES" to these three questions that you can begin to step toward seeing fruit in your marriage.

Today! The psalmist said, "Your word is a lamp for my feet, a light on my path" (Psalm 119:105).

So we get it, it's all You, God. You are good and faithful and have plans to protect and prosper our marriage and give it a future.

Today, why don't you spend the day focusing on your walk with the Lord, even before focusing on your marriage? Think about His love for you and the future He planned for you as He went to the cross. Think about when you first cried out for His forgiveness and that feeling of love and joy pouring into your heart. What experiences have you had where He has shown Himself faithful, getting you through tough situations and into new seasons in your life?

Maybe you're reading this but you have never been forgiven for your sins. Maybe you have never repented—meaning that you've never turned away from the life you were living and asked God to forgive you through Jesus' sacrifice and resurrection. Romans 10:9 tells us, "if you confess with your mouth the Lord Jesus and believe in your heart that God has raised Him from the dead, you will be saved" (NKJV). That's it—a work of God as we confess Him as Lord.

You see, this book can't save you. I can't save you. A church, a pastor, or anyone else, for that matter, can't save you. Only Jesus can save you. Period. You can go to Him today, right now, lay your life before Him in thankfulness, and praise Him for His love toward you. And as a reality check, as amazing as a restored marriage is and what God may go on to do in your marriage, as you get to the end of your life and stand before the Lord, would you value your marriage above the gift of eternal life?

Today, think about how awesome your Shepherd is and what He has done. Hear His voice calling you to do great things. Do you know His voice? Do you know Him? I pray you do.

DAY 3: PERSPECTIVE IS REALITY! OR IS IT?

Day three; we now know that God poured His love out on us even when we were unlovable. He gave us a spouse—another human, one of His sheep—to love unconditionally. So today, it is of the utmost importance for us to understand that this earth, where we abide, is a cursed world.

There are good things that happen here. You may help an old lady across the street. You may not tell that person what you really think. You may even go out of your way to serve others. But since "the fall" in the garden, people, whether they know it or not, consciously or unconsciously, have been looking for a way to be set free from the curse (Romans 8:19–21).

As I connect with people, one of the main things I have seen that keeps them from growing in their faith is that they don't fully understand the world we live in.

On day one, we saw how we were fooled into thinking love was something it isn't. We can also view this world, experience it, and comprehend it as something it really isn't. By this I mean, why did my mother just pass away? Why did my wife miscarry our fourth child whom we had seen skipping and jumping in the womb and had already been named? *Wow, why so direct, Brian?* Because we have to understand the world for what it is. Though these two events were tragic and life-changing, did God not know these events would happen beforehand? Did He not send His Son to give us peace in this world even at times when we might not fully understand? The Bible says that we only "know in part," after all (1 Corinthians 13:9).

While some can get mad at God, turn away from Him, and even say they hate God, I have to believe that as my baby girl graduated from this world and entered into eternity, she got to meet her grandmother, my mother, Norma Jean, in heaven. Do you see His perspective in these situations? His reality?

Understanding God's perspective through our salvation in Jesus Christ is what saves us from missing the point. He has a higher purpose for everything that happens. We accept and ultimately come to understand this through our faith in Him.

Understanding and applying this principle alone will enable you to see everything together as a married couple, from here on out, to be subject to His purpose, His plan, His will. The world is a crazy place. People are being lied to, cheated on, martyred (killed), and so much more. Without His perspective on the things we encounter in life, the alternative is … well … crazy.

One of the most popular verses carved onto wall plaques, on refrigerator magnets, or underlined in Bibles is from Paul's letter to the Romans. He writes "And we know that all things work together for good to those who love God, to those who are the called according to His purpose" (8:28, NKJV). We love this, right? It sounds so great. Everything is going to end up GOOD for us. Perfect! Yet, we don't seem to piece together that just ten verses earlier, in the same letter, Paul writes on his current condition: "For I consider that the sufferings of this present time are not worthy to be compared with the glory which shall be revealed in us" (8:18, NKJV). Sufferings? Present time? What was he facing—as a Christian?

Sadly, the Gospel message we so often receive is that the world is centered on us. So, is it any wonder that we feel everything should be handed to us on a silver platter? We see Job as a book of suffering, yet in the beginning Satan shows up, wagering, if you like, against God. He challenges God that if Job loses his livestock, property, family, and is afflicted, he will turn and curse the Lord. What is more amazing is that God is the one who nominates Job, saying, "Have you considered my servant Job?" (Job 1:8) And get this! God is the one who grants Satan the permission to afflict him!

So is the book of Job about suffering, or is it about God getting all of the glory from Job despite his situation? Is my marriage about me and my wife, foremost, or is it about our witness for the Lord as we face the storms or trials of life together?

Paul said the sufferings of this present time are "not worthy to be compared with the glory which shall be revealed in us." *Revealed in us!* That God would use us, shape us, and guide us. Yes, that's exactly what He does! If we put Romans 8:28 alongside the sufferings of Paul in Romans 8:18 and take our lives and situations here on this earth, honestly asking why we face the hardships, struggles, and the challenges, He answers us directly, solidly, and lovingly with this verse: "For those God foreknew he also predestined to be conformed to the image of his Son, that he might be the firstborn among many brothers and sisters" (Romans 8:29). Friends, we are being made, conformed, and changed into someone's image daily. If we are following Christ, it is His image that we are being conformed into. He is the Potter. We are clay!

I hope you see that everything is ordained and allowed by God. You woke up this morning; the sun beamed in through the window; that breath you just took; every little detail is held together by Him. Knowing this and seeing this world for what it is will allow every challenge you face to be another witness of how He is in control and how He is there for you, no matter what the world may throw at you.

Our greatest example and advocate is Jesus. And even He, the Messiah, while kneeling in the Garden of Gethsemane, cried out to God the Father, showing His human condition, sweating blood, and asking that if it were possible that the cup He was about to drink be taken away. That cup, which represented our sins, the wrath we deserve and our place on the cross, could not be dealt with any other way. Here we see true love at work. It was in Jesus' greatest hardships, His betrayal, and His journey to and death on the cross that we see the greatest of love. We often hear the saying, "It was not the nails that held Him there," and how true that is. It was love, it was hardship, it was seeing the state of the world for what it is and doing what must be done. Jesus was willing to do His Father's will, despite the pain, despite the cost.

Consider and share with your partner today:

1. An event from your past (together and/or as individuals) where you handled things in a way that DIDN'T glorify God.

2. An event from your past (together and/or as individuals) where you handled things in a way that DID glorify God.

3. An event you are experiencing today where you have an opportunity to handle it in a way that will glorify God. Are you ready?

Remember, He said, "I will never leave you nor forsake you" (Hebrews 13:5, NKJV), and "We must through many tribulations enter the kingdom of God" (Acts 14:22, NKJV).

God is aware of each and every experience you will face in the world. Are you prepared to make sure the world sees His light reflected through your response? Or will they view you as another hypocrite/worldly Christian who can't handle things and lets the things of this world get to them?

Remember Hebrews 4:15–16:

For we do not have a high priest who is unable to empathize with our weaknesses, but we have one who has been tempted in every way, just as we are—yet he did not sin. Let us then approach God's throne of grace with confidence, so that we may receive mercy and find grace to help us in our time of need.

Christ has been there and done that. Follow His example so that when tough times arise, you can go to God with confidence that you "may receive mercy and find grace to help us in our time of need."

Life is going to throw some curveballs at us, but in Christ we have already hit a homerun. Make sure you have this perspective as you start this journey for your marriage.

DAY 4: WE SAID "WE DO." NOW WHAT?

Coming to America around the age of fifteen to skateboard, I didn't know the next few years would entail trips back and forth across the pond, falling in love with America and an American named Tracy, who had an accent and even drove on the wrong side of the road. Though she did, it didn't stop me from riding shotgun in her car that next day, unbeknownst to both our families, all in the name of love.

She said "yes. Let's do it! We will drive out to Vegas and get married tomorrow!"

We have already addressed that our view of love is tainted, and that God's love is the only true, unconditional love. So what about marriage? In our sinful state of not having a clue about what we were getting into by saying "I do," was anything of God on display in that?

Years later, as I sat reading the creation story in Genesis—before there was sin, before there was pain and hurt, and before our world needed saving—all seemed to be good in the garden. In fact, we read that God Himself "saw that it was good," yet suddenly out of nowhere, God puts things on hold and lets us know that something "is not good" (Genesis 2:18). Sounds good to me. No death, lying, cheating, selfishness, blasphemy, so what isn't good? God expounds: "It is not good that man should be alone" (NKJV). *Alone? But man is not alone. He is hanging out with You, God. You are everything and more than enough. You sustain the universe. You are our provider, deliverer, healer, and so much more. Adam has all he needs. And God, You have already said it was good.*

Yet, right there in the beginning, right before we ever see sin or the need for redemption, do you see what God had in mind? Man was missing something, or rather someone; he was without his woman! "I will make him a helper fit for him" (ESV). Here we go!

Now out of the ground the LORD God had formed every beast of the field and every bird of the heavens and brought them to the man to see what he would call them. ... The man gave names to all livestock and to the birds of the heavens and to every beast of the field. But for Adam there was not found a helper fit for him.

Genesis 2:19–20, ESV

Don't know about you, but praise God for that. God could have designed our "helper" and spouse to look however or be whatever. Here we see Him actually bringing the animals to Adam, so you could have ended up marrying a pig. Hopefully not. But God was making the point that in all God had created, there was no helper that could live up to or have that special mystique that Adam needed.

So the LORD God caused a deep sleep to fall upon the man, and while he slept took one of his ribs and closed up its place with flesh. And the rib that the LORD God had taken from the man he made into a woman and brought her to the man.

Genesis 2:21–22, ESV

Intro you, wife! There you are. Wonderfully and fearfully made, and on purpose, with a purpose, by a purposeful God. Imagine if women just got this point alone. If the covers of our magazines or the topics of the most popular talk shows glorified how a woman is made special, and without her, man is missing part of himself. That she came from out of his "rib," and that's right where she belongs—beneath his arm, tucked in, warm and cozy. Ladies, you get to be the expression of God's intention for womanhood.

Even here in this passage, talking about Adam's sleep (trance), note that in the very beginning, the woman was "one" with Adam. She was part of him, from his innermost parts. The Hebrew word for "rib" is a feminine noun relating to cell structure; it is even used elsewhere in reference to the structure of the temple. Just a few passages later, God pronounces them "one flesh" (verse 24), or to use New Testament pictures, we could say "one temple," similar to how God's Spirit dwells today inside believers. We can conclude from this word that the woman is an imperative part of the structure of a couple.

Getting back to the picture of creation, consider Adam's thoughts as God displayed all of the animals to him. Remember, God Himself had said that it wasn't good for man to be alone and that He Himself would make a helper fit for him. After looking at the cows, goats, giraffes, and snakes, just to name a few, he was probably questioning if God was feeling okay that day. But I am sure his shock soon turned to joy as his eyes first made contact with Eve's. *God, You've done it. You've mastered it! Thank You, God. You have given me a woman.*

God didn't need to bring him a selection of women, just one. One was all it took for Adam's life to be forever changed, as we begin to see his romantic side unfold and we hear the first recorded poem:

> Then the man said, "This at last is bone of my bones and flesh of my flesh; she shall be called Woman, because she was taken out of Man." Therefore a man shall leave his father and his mother and hold fast to his wife, and they shall become one flesh. And the man and his wife were both naked and were not ashamed.
>
> *Genesis 2:23–24, ESV*

There is it—marriage. Adam and his wife Eve, becoming one. She takes his last name, puts on his ring, and upon physical consummation (sex), there is a shedding of blood, confirming the covenant. Amazing. And Adam even cries out "at last."

God said it was bad that man was alone, so He made it good. He gave Adam a helper, a best friend, a lover, a partner, a wife!

Of all the things we think we know about marriage, how amazing it is to remember that Genesis, the book of origins, begins with the marriage of Adam and Eve; and the book of Revelation, the consummation of all things, ends with the marriage of Christ and His bride, the church.

Did you know that the story of the Bible, in a nutshell, is about a prince (Jesus) who overcomes the works of a dragon (Satan) in order that He might redeem and marry His wife (the church/you and me)?

In Genesis and throughout the Old Testament, we see marriage lived out, but it is in Paul's letter to the church in Ephesus that we are told the mystery of marriage.

> Therefore a man shall leave his father and mother and hold fast to his wife, and the two shall become one flesh. This mystery is profound, and I am saying that it refers to Christ and the church.
>
> *Ephesians 5:31–32, ESV*

As we said "I do" that night, we had no idea of the beauty and mystery God had planned to display as we entered into the amazing covenant of marriage. We allowed all that we had seen in the world to define what a marriage should be. Thanks, Hollywood. And though we tried, we weren't putting God first. In fact, He was an afterthought. At the time, we were the gods of our lives.

However, many marriages fail, not because of people's view of marriage, but because of their views of God. Remember, marriage (after the cross) is the greatest representation here on earth of the love Christ has for the church/His bride. Therefore, live, love, and make your marriage a display and an example to the world of Christ's love. If you seek to do that, everything about your marriage will be different.

You're on day four of our thirty days. Are you still listening to Jesus' voice in everything that has been shared to this point? There is a light ahead, so let's keep pressing in.

By now your perspective should be beginning to change in reference to your view on life and marriage. Maybe its upside down right now—times are tough; you don't know what to do; and you don't feel like it can be fixed. Maybe it's going great, and this was just a bump of encouragement. Whatever the situation, I have a few thoughts for you.

Men: Do you see that God brought you one wife, and God is never wrong? How are you covering her, loving her, and looking out for her?

Women: Do you see that God made you out of man, your place is alongside him, and you were made to be his helper? I love the thought that after the Holy Spirit, my wife is the best helper I can have here on this earth.

I understand that you may have a spouse who isn't reading this book with you, who doesn't want to hear about it, and may even be trying to leave the relationship, having possibly fallen into sin. Please, today, be the best you can be for the Lord, and love your spouse as unto God.

First Peter 3:7 says, "husbands, live with your wives in an understanding way" (ESV). Not just if she is doing things as you or the Lord would like, but as your spouse, love her unconditionally, understanding where she is, believing for the best.

Proverbs 31:12 "She brings him good, not harm, all the days of her life." Wives, today, simply treating your husband as best as you can for the Lord will be a witness to him and will show him your love.

DAY 5: THE COVENANT OF ONE FLESH

Our marriage is of God. He designed it, blessed it, and has made Himself accountable for it. A good marriage is one of the blessings we can enjoy because of Christ's death on the cross. But we often view God as so remote—not part of our daily lives—that we don't walk with Him daily through the ins and outs of our marriage.

Let me ask you what it was that united you two as you said, "I do"? Was it because you were in a church? The vows that were spoken? The people in attendance? The pastor? We could go on and on, but it wasn't any of those things. It was God! God Himself who formed us from the dust of the earth and breathed life into us. He formed your union and did the miraculous work of making two become one. Only God can do this work of cleaving. Your marriage is a miracle. Do you think of it that way today?

Now, my wife and I have individual thoughts. We may want to parent our kids in different ways at times. Our ideas about where to vacation may be different. But our whole life is lived out with the idea that God views us as one, and we function best when we strive to live in unity—as one.

When the Pharisees asked Jesus what His thoughts on divorce were, quoting that Moses had "permitted a man to write a certificate of divorce and send [his wife] away" (Mark 10:4), Jesus answered by taking them back to Genesis, giving them God's intention (Mark 10:5–9):

> "It was because your hearts were hard that Moses wrote you this law," Jesus replied. "But at the beginning of creation God 'made them male and female.' 'For this reason a man will leave his father and mother and be united to his wife, and the two will become one flesh.' So they are no longer two, but one flesh. Therefore what God has joined together, let no one separate."

What God has done, He who joined them, let no man separate! But their hearts were hard. They hadn't been saved. They didn't have the Holy Spirit. And they didn't have access to God the way we do today. Romans 5:20 says, "Where sin increased, grace increased all the more," speaking of the grace we have access to today to overcome sin and not be so hardhearted.

I've seen many couples face hard times, serious disconnection, disagreements, and even infidelity. Yet, I still counsel them to do all that they can, by God's power, to make it work, to begin to live for Him. God has performed miracles, and He will not take His hand off your marriage as you keep turning to Him.

If there is confession, repentance, and a commitment to following Christ, even if there has been infidelity, a godly marriage is possible if the offended spouse can forgive. Your marriage may be the worst it has ever been, and maybe this book is your last hope, but I can say with all confidence that the pastor, facilitator, and Father of you both, God Almighty, is still for you. He will give you a future and a hope (Jeremiah 29:11).

Power of Covenant

The reason He is for you is because your marriage is not only a covenant between you and your spouse, but with God. Today, the world views the vows and ceremony, even the layout of the church, as traditional. It's far from that. It's a demonstration of covenant.

When God said "yes" to our marriage, He said *yes* to a covenant, a forever commitment. But in most marriages today, people are often just saying yes to a contract; there is a big difference.

A contract, by definition, protects each member of the agreement. If you and I sign a contract for you to fix my garage, upon finishing it, I am also contracted to pay you what we agreed. A contract looks out for you, guaranteeing that as long as you do your part, I will do mine. We have an agreement. We often view our marriages in that same way. We view what our spouses should be doing as keeping to the contract.

But a covenant in marriage says regardless of what you do, I am going to love you and keep my commitment. God's covenant says that though you were born in sin, He sent Jesus to save you. Regardless of you bailing in the garden or your rebellion in the Old Testament, He lived and died for you. Covenant says, "I will be your God and you will be My people; I will never leave you nor forsake you" (see Leviticus 26:12 and Joshua 1:5).

You see, we stand before our family members and friends on our wedding day, dressed in our perfect suits, fulfilling childhood dreams, reciting our vows, and looking into our future. Yet sadly, once the romance and emotions fade, we default to the contract we made, not the covenant that only God's love can enable us to keep. Do you see how even our idea of marriage is contractual, as opposed to covenantal?

I never wanted to divorce my wife, but we were living on contractual terms, based on what we expected of one another. When we finally failed each other enough times, turned our heads in other directions, and because there was no covenant, we both gave in and each found an out in our "contract."

It's here that the words of Proverbs and Malachi would have spoken to us. May they speak to you today:

" ... who has left the partner of her youth and ignored the covenant she made before God."

Proverbs 2:17

You ask, "Why?" It is because the LORD is the witness between you and the wife of your youth. You have been unfaithful to her, though she is your partner, the wife of your marriage covenant.

Malachi 2:14

We could have stepped back and said, *Yes, this is tough. Yes, everything doesn't make sense to us, but we serve a God of covenant, a God who is still here and eager to see this thing through.* If we had focused on the covenant, our marriage would have made it through, guaranteed. This isn't just an observation—this is a fact.

You see, one of the things about God's marriage covenant is this: even though we are included and we can add our two cents, so to speak, His covenants, as far as His helping us, are always with Himself. We are not really part of the equation. Since God is all-knowing, He knew that Tracy and I would fail each other and would see divorce as the way out. But He made a covenant with Himself to eagerly be available to help us. Yes, the God of all things is eager to honor His covenant today.

We see a picture of this covenant relationship in the Old Testament. God promised Abraham that He would grant him a child and even land to possess. And although we see many people who doubt throughout the pages of Scripture, it is when a person believes that we see God most glorified in their lives. Genesis 15:6 says, "Abram believed the LORD, and he credited it to him as righteousness." What was it that Abraham believed? He knew God was a just God—a God who keeps His covenants, one who never breaks His promises.

Going back to our story in Genesis, we see God setting the scene. He tells Abraham to lay various animas out and cut them in half. Then, "When the sun had set and darkness had fallen, a smoking firepot with a blazing torch appeared and passed between the pieces. On that day the LORD made a covenant with Abram" (Genesis 15:17–18). God shows up between the animals, treads the bloodline, and takes the responsibility, so should anything happen, the consequences fall on Him.

God did this for our marriage. As two families sat on either side, we walked the aisle between them, a bloodline if you like, binding them, a passing of a surname, a unity, bonding. "One Flesh" being formed. What's different for our marriage covenant is that we walked this bloodline with God, making ourselves accountable for what happens. "Ouch!" You guessed it! Just as the animals were cut in two, the ancient idea was that should we break the covenant, what was done to these animals should be done to us. Or, as Jesus put it, "Therefore what God has joined together, let no one separate" (Mark 10:9).

God has not given up and will not give up on your marriage because God cannot lie. He saw that it was bad that man was alone, so He brought Adam a wife and blessed the marriage. He is still in covenant with believers because in making this covenant, He didn't swear by what you would do, but what He would do. Hebrews 6:13 says, "When God made his promise to Abraham, since there was no one greater for him to swear by, he swore by himself." He swore by Himself, made a covenant with Himself to be there for your marriage, as you walk in this covenant with God.

The fact that you are in covenant with both God and your spouse should help you to eradicate such words as divorce or separation. It should help you automatically do away with things and situations that you would treat like conditions in a contract. In the story of the great flood, did God shine His rainbow as evidence He wouldn't flood the earth again because of something Noah did? In any of the gospels, did Jesus say He chose us based upon our jumping through hoops to gain salvation? God is for your marriage and nothing can stop that, but that doesn't mean you guys can't stop your marriage, give up on covenant, and fall into the contractual relationship again.

Again, today, take some time to ask yourselves these questions:

1. Have you put upon your spouse any rules or conditions, like a contract, that are hindering your covenant?

2. Are you aware that every day God intends to be part of every area of your marriage, and it's His covenant power that will sustain you?

Be energetic in your life of salvation, reverent and sensitive before God. That energy is God's energy, an energy deep within you, God himself willing and working at what will give him the most pleasure.

Philippians 2:13, THE MESSAGE

Spend some time with your spouse in prayer, giving things over to the Lord, confessing where you are, and asking Him to be the center of this marriage covenant. **Do it today.**

DAY 6: THE "F" WORD = FORGIVENESS

Bear with each other and forgive one another if any of you has a grievance against someone. Forgive as the Lord forgave you.

Colossians 3:13

Wow, how different would the world be if everyone chose to forgive? Would the Beatles have stayed together a few years longer (hopefully going on to become a worship band)? Would Morrissey and Marr have found more meaning to the Smiths' song, "There is a light that never goes out"? Who knows? But if forgiveness was chosen more often, we know families would remain together longer, countries would fight less, and there would be less bitterness and hurt in the world.

Is there really anything greater we can address, after God's love for us, than His forgiveness toward us? Even in that love, it was His choosing to forgive us that we saw and felt His love at work. It was the evidence of His love, for that matter. He saw our state, and rather than hold on, be bitter, and be let down, He, by His nature, forgave. In fact, because He's God, even before He made us, He knew we would fail and that we would need to be forgiven. This tells us that the perfect thing to do, because He is perfect, is to forgive just as Jesus demonstrated.

As I sit here in bed, Tracy beside me reading her devotional, I have to say that I have more to reflect on these days than I ever imagined. Thirty-four years of age, after thirteen years of marriage thus far, one thing we really needed to learn was to choose to forgive. There are stories upon stories about things we have said, done, and fallen into that have caused Tracy and me to need to forgive one another over and over again. Knowing our ongoing need to be forgiven, both by our spouses and others in this world, there will always be situations where we will need to ask for and receive forgiveness. Therefore, we need to be willing to show grace and forgiveness.

To take this to the extreme, I remember one night getting an email from a couple I had seen around town who had caught some of our marriage story based on my Facebook posts. Their email to me that night ended with "urgent!"

When I called, I expected the worst, and I was right. She had been caught in the midst of an affair. In a situation with another man, her husband returned home; their kids were asleep, and she was with a best friend.

As I hurried to Starbucks to meet them the next day, I knew two things. She was repentant, and he was forgiving. She had come clean, and he had chosen to forgive.

Pulling up, with them looking like two wet dogs out in the rain, shaking with anxiety, on the edge of being shattered, I have to say walking over to them I felt the joy of the Lord.

"Do you know that for you to have come clean and to have repented," I told her, "and for you to be willing to forgive," I told the husband, "you have opened the door for the Lord to get glory out of your relationship?" Tears came down his face, as he smiled and cried at once, pulling her in closer, trying to be the strength in this relationship with whatever life he had left.

"Forgive her?" his friends asked. "Stay with her?" "Trust her again?" While they have every worldly reason to say this, to think this, and to expect this, one thing that they will witness in his forgiving is that no one in the entire world can ever forgive her the way her husband is choosing to aside from Jesus!

Because God has brought them together and miraculously made them "one flesh," there is no one else alive that can forgive in any way greater than that of a spouse. Who in the entire world can ever forgive this woman more than the husband whom she had betrayed? No one! He's been violated, wounded, and mistreated by his special helper, and yet, as he turns to God—does it God's way—we again see the love of Christ: powerful, majestic, and wonderfully on display for so many to see. Even here in these pages.

While people may see him as weak and a fool, I see him as strong and courageous. While the world may say *move on and seek that which is better*, he is aware that "love covers a multitude of sins" (1 Peter 4:8, ESV). And, contrary to popular belief, people do grow and change. Yes, they really can; not just you. Hard to believe, but true.

This couple walked through a time of confession, repentance, discussion, and healing. Then they set boundaries because both of them were now aware of the enemy's attacks and the weakness of the flesh. But of all these things, in order for them to move on, it will be on his choosing to forgive and forget.

I get it though: it hurts, it's wrong, it's not what was planned. But in your marriage, you will find that living with anyone born into sin, though they are growing into the image of Christ (Romans 8:29), there will still be situations that require forgiveness. Everything from fights about the way the toilet paper faces, the time the kids go to bed, when to be physical, where to eat (especially where to eat, actually), and beyond.

You see, the thing about forgiveness is that it really isn't about them. Yes, they may have said this and that, done this and even done *that*, but forgiveness is really about you and the Lord. I am not saying that what anyone did was okay, but I am saying this: why are you the one walking around carrying it while they are off on their merry way? God tells us to *forgive, even as Christ forgave us* (Ephesians 4:32). And what's amazing in the Greek is, He meant it. Even as "Christ." While being hated, lied about, beaten, whipped, spat upon, nailed to a cross, and left to die, He still kept His focus and accomplished His God-sent goal. "For the joy was set before him, he endured the cross" (Hebrews 12:2). He did this because, not only was He sent in the flesh by God, but He also chose to forgive while we were still unaware of it and in our own little sinful world, like the one you or your spouse may seem to be living in at times (John 1:14; Romans 5:8; Luke 23:34).

I am not writing this book to tell you how to make your marriage perfect; I am writing this book to tell you how going through life with God as the head and walking in His ways and glorifying Him will enable your marriage to be perfected DAILY by Him!

I am not here to approve of adultery. God hates it, and it is a destroyer of many homes. But I am here to tell you that what is more powerful than pain, hurt, adultery, and any other sin is forgiveness. And we must choose to forgive, again and again! When Peter came to Jesus, in his boldness he asked the question "Lord, how many times shall I forgive my brother or sister who sins against me?" It's amazing—Peter doesn't let Jesus answer, but instead answers himself, possibly implying "I'm so holy; I am willing to forgive even 'up to seven times'" (see Matthew 18:21). Yet, Jesus set the record straight, saying, "not seven times, but seventy-seven times" (verse 22).

That's an awful lot! Yet Jesus wasn't saying to keep track and forgive only 490 times but that we need to continue to forgive.

Without Christ, I would tell a couple that it is going to be next to impossible for their marriage to make it. Only thirty percent of marriages ever survive after such circumstances. But with Christ, with true forgiveness and through God's love, "all things are possible" (Matthew 19:26).

Talking about forgiveness, as you think about it, do you really understand it? First Corinthians 13:5 says love "keeps no records of wrongs." No record? No account? No bringing it up? No holding on? No reminding? No using it to make one feel guilty or to manipulate? Yes! Just as God forgave us and remembers our sins no more (Isaiah 43:25), we are to forgive as well. It isn't that God is forgetful. He is God, aware of everything, perfect. No, it's that God chooses *not* to remember. He made the choice and keeps making the choice to forget, and that's where we are today.

I don't know the life you've lived, the things you've faced, or even the state of your marriage. I do know about who created us and in whose image we are made. I remember coming to understand that my wife was first and foremost a child of God, a sinner saved by grace, and His constant work of art, *then*, my wife. Though I would hope and pray she would do me no wrong or harm, I also must realize that God is at work in her, that He knew I would be her husband, and that I am going to play one of the starring roles in His forming and shaping her. After all, we are "one flesh."

It's with this foundation and understanding that I can look at her on the hardest of days, and her at me, and we can say, "God, though my flesh feels off, and though I would choose to do this a different way, I am choosing to take steps of faith, trusting in You and letting go of everything, big or small, that may be causing me to view Your child through a bitter heart, with gnashing teeth, or even clenched fists." There will be ups and downs, slammed doors, loud voices, and more. But the way to get further and further down the road of unity and harmony is by making the choice to forgive one another, "even as God in Christ forgave you" (Ephesians 4:32, NKJV). Making the choice to forgive will change your marriage and stop so many future catastrophes.

In relation to the issue of forgiveness, here's a few questions for you and your spouse to prayerfully answer:

1. What am I holding on to that is causing me to be more shaped into the image of my old self rather than the image of Christ?

2. Who do I need to forgive and release today?

3. Am I able to not look back, but from this point on, choose to forgive what wrongs may have been done?

Consider that the apostle Paul made a big deal of one of the things he did.

But one thing I do: forgetting what lies behind and straining forward to what lies ahead, I press on toward the goal for the prize of the upward call of God in Christ Jesus.

Philippians 3:13–14, ESV

DAY 7: WORKMANSHIP / SERVANTHOOD

We left off last time talking about forgiveness—how it is about us, not what someone else has done to us. Letting go of the past and staying focused on Christ, moving forward.

During a recent time of on-and-off ministry around America, sharing my testimony and God's Word, I saw a consistent pattern again and again.

As I arrived at each town, almost everywhere I went, I would meet with someone who was at a dead end in their life. Be it the girl who asked me to sign her arm, and upon grabbing her sharpie to do so, I was met with cuts from her wrist to elbow, as if I wouldn't notice. Yes, she was this comfortable!

Or the girl the next night who was offered pills her whole life by her mother. Her mother hoping she would end her life, eventually going on to stab her; then after the mother sent her to stay with the dad, the father put the girl's head through a window, throwing her idea of love and family into a whirlwind of hurt at the age of fourteen.

Another night, after a young man's father had passed away, he could barely look people in the eye. He was anxious and shaken, struggling with life and loss.

Then finally, the last night in Texas, in the midst of a giant skateboard competition, after just hearing the Gospel, a guy who was so depressed and anxious that he could barely stand sought prayer and counsel to overcome suicidal thoughts, all because of an old girlfriend.

If you were approached by one of these people, what exactly would you have shared with them in those moments? What exactly can I possibly say, pray, or write to them later that will redirect and have a lasting effect on their lives? What would you say?

The reason I believe so many of these people are in the midst of an ocean on a sinking ship, or living their days while life happens *to* them rather than making life happen, is because they are missing their purpose.

When I connected with each of these people while out on the road, at the skate park, in the chapel, or in the parking lot, I wanted them to grasp one specific truth:

> For we are His workmanship, created in Christ Jesus for good works, which God prepared beforehand that we should walk in them.
>
> *Ephesians 2:10, NKJV*

Such a familiar verse, but do we really consider this great truth? Are we laying it down as a foundation for life and getting it inside of us? Paul, speaking by the Holy Spirit to the church in Ephesus, said, "We are." Not *we are trying to be,* not *we are hoping to be,* but "we are." We are *what*? "His workmanship." Listen, you "are His workmanship, created in Christ Jesus for good works." Before you were even formed and created, before you had ever sinned, God had in mind your blueprint and the things you were called to do in this life. He knew Adam and Eve would sin, He knew you would be born into sin, and He knew He would send Jesus to change all of that. But before all of this, He designed you with a purpose.

In the same way someone took a piece of wood and shaped and crafted it, birthing the skateboard, so you were shaped. In the same way someone considered a screw and made a drill with the ability to drill, so you were made. And we could go on with a guitar, a boat, a paintbrush, a pair of shoes, whatever.

And if these things are not doing what they were designed and made for, they are either sitting around wasting away or being used for the wrong things. Wow, that sounds convicting. But there is a reason Jesus said, "whoever does not gather with me scatters" (Matthew 12:30).

My point, in a nutshell, is that when you remember that every day, God has given you the exact amount of time needed to breathe, live, and accomplish what He has called you to, this driving force will change your whole life and perspective. Not only will it help to accomplish God's purposes in you, but it will also protect you from falling into harm's way, and by that I mean remaining stagnant or worse. There is biblical truth to the saying, "idle hands are the devil's workshop." And boy, is he excited to help you use your gifts and talents for evil.

We always make claims like, "there is never enough time." But I can I tell you—there is exactly enough time. Jesus is the "author and finisher of our faith" (Hebrews 12:2, NKJV), and you are not leaving this earth until He decides. He gave us the abilities needed, the gifts necessary, and His grace, mercy, and the power of the Holy Spirit to get us through this life.

In my travels, I meet many people, and for every one of us, life has its ups and downs. It rains "on the just and on the unjust" (Matthew 5:45, NKJV); but we are here each day, and God is with us to accomplish His purpose.

Paul said, "God prepared" these works "beforehand that we should walk in them" (Ephesians 2:10, NKJV). Daily, at all times.

That's why we see a shepherd boy called David out in the fields dancing as he tends his father's sheep and crying out to his God in songs of praise and worship, able to overcome lions, bears, and even going on to kill and destroy a giant Philistine named Goliath, who had put the fear of hell into King Saul's army. With just a slingshot and a few smooth stones, he became the greatest of heroes to the Hebrew nation. What was so different about David? Wasn't he just a human like any other? Yes, but he knew his calling; he knew the works God had given to him to "walk in" each day.

In the same way, every person ever created, including us and our spouses and the people we read about in the Bible, were made on purpose, *for a purpose*. When we wake each morning to live for Christ, with His purpose in mind, we will steer clear of all the distractions and hiccups. Those kids I met, those shattered couples, you who are reading this book: Have you taken inventory of your life and asked God, "What have You called me to do? What is my purpose?"

Those who look at their lives, families, situations, and marriages, and say, "God, what is my work? What is the workmanship You have given me to do? How is the time You have allotted for me every day to be spent?" will receive an answer.

It is my belief that those who honestly ask these questions will truly understand their purpose. Jesus came to die for our sins that we might "Go into all the world and proclaim the gospel to the whole creation" (Mark 16:15, ESV). But we must be filled with the Holy Spirit, God's literal presence inside of us, that we might go into all the world. Jesus said, "But you will receive power when the Holy Spirit has come upon you, and you will be my witnesses in Jerusalem and in all Judea and Samaria, and to the end of the earth" (Acts 1:8, ESV).

But I must mention this: even King David, "a man after his own heart" (1 Samuel 13:14), later on in his life, after serving God, winning many battles, and becoming king, was radically changed forever because he was not walking in the "work" God had created him for. Second Samuel 11:1 tells us, "At the time when kings go off to war, David sent Joab." Oh he did? That was nice. Did you catch that? David was king, and this was the time "kings go off to war," yet this king decided not to go.

He decided that someone else could do the work given to him. And as he sat, lounging around on his rooftop, maybe heating up the Jacuzzi, playing some mini golf, or getting high scores on the newest video games, his gaze fell on Bathsheba, the wife of his loyal friend, Uriah. He lusts. He cheats. He has Uriah assassinated. Bathsheba is pregnant and the baby dies. Wow! All this death from one sin! How it could have been avoided? If he had lived that day, doing what he was called to do, being God's "workmanship, created in Christ Jesus for good works," and going "to war," this great sin, which gave occasion to the enemies of the Lord to blaspheme, would not have occurred.

This may sound so simple, but knowing you are made for a purpose can keep you from the nothings that strive for our attention every day. The girl I recently met, who was done living because she didn't have enough friends, will see as she lives purposefully for Christ, knowing her purpose, that she will meet and bond with friends who are believers. For us as couples, having entered into a marriage covenant, we get to look to one another and slow the world down, saying, *What am I to do? How can I help my spouse accomplish what they were made for?*

Peter called us a "chosen generation, a royal priesthood, a holy nation" (1 Peter 2:9, NKJV), blessing us and telling us that in the Old Testament, God's presence was only in some believers, but today, His presence is in all believers.

When Jesus was on the cross and the ground shook and quaked open, the Bible makes it clear the temple veil was torn. In the Old Testament, only the high priest could go behind that veil once a year to speak with God on behalf of the people. But today, we have His presence inside each of us, and we should look forward to living each day to manifest Him. Imagine if Jesus could walk alongside us every day, leading and directing us exactly where to go. Would we be eager to do the work allotted to us each day because we would feel His presence with us? Yet, what's even more amazing is He told us "it is to your advantage that I go away, for if I do not go away, the Helper will not come to you. But if I go, I will send him to you" (John 16:7, ESV).

How amazing is that truth? He went away that the Holy Spirit might come and lead us.

1. God has called you to *Go*, meaning you should live for Him each day, pointing to who He is in everything. Ask yourself and your spouse: are you both ready to work together to live a life of *going*?

2. What are the works He has called you to do? Jesus was called to walk on water, but I am not. I am called to share, write this book, love on people, and use my gifts. What about you?

3. What can you and your spouse do better together that will help encourage one another's *work*?

DAY 8: HIS PART

As we step into day eight, hopefully you have discovered some things from God's Word that have helped to structure where your marriage is going. He has a plan for your marriage and wants to guide you into what may be just around the corner. Around the corner begins right now. As a couple, this is the time to take what we know of God and why His Spirit lives inside of us, and together, step into the task. Jesus said, "If a house is divided against itself, that house cannot stand" (Mark 3:25). A house—its foundation, structure, pillars, the nuts and bolts, the blueprint. We can take this verse and apply it directly to our marriages, to our walks, to our oneness. We could even suggest that if a marriage is divided, it cannot stand. Though two people can stay together, and though one could make the effort, sooner or later, the division will grow deeper and deeper, and one may well leave.

It's important to lay the foundation; and ladies, whatever way you see this, the foundation laid by God begins with *man*. That doesn't mean women are any less, or that God didn't have a plan in which He knew man would be without woman. It just means that God did it this way, so let's hear Him out before half the feminists in the world have a meltdown. Yes, He made them male and female in Genesis 1, but in Genesis 2 we see that God put Adam in the garden and told him "to tend and keep it" (Genesis 2:15, NKJV). God then went on to tell Adam, not to "eat from the tree" (Genesis 2:17), for in that day they would surely die. Everything was good in the garden, aside from the fact that man was "alone" (Genesis 2:18). God made Adam the perfect "helper," woman, his wife, and Adam's job was to love her, cover her, and protect her. She came from him, and as part of him, was one with him.

What's amazing to me when reading the creation story is we jump into Genesis 3 and we suddenly see the "serpent" conversing with Eve and challenging her trust in what God has said. "Has God indeed said, 'You shall not eat of every tree of the garden'?" (Genesis 3:1, NKJV). It was Adam that God gave direction to, so how was Eve deceived? Was Adam doing his part, listening to God, watching out for Eve, covering her?

Men, I want to challenge you right here and now, even while your wife reads along and she may even be tempted to say "I told you so." In your walk with God, there is no greater human to care for and love than your wife. At the end of your life, of all the kids you have raised, jobs you have had, money you have made, projects you have finished, places visited, albums sold, movies you may have made, planets you have landed on, diseases you may have found cures for, I can promise you, nothing will be more important than how you loved and walked alongside your wife.

It's a fact because our marriage is a picture of Christ and His bride, the church. He showed the highest level of love, He gave His very best—Himself— to cover her, watch out for her, and protect her. Paul reveals this mystery when, in writing to the church in Ephesus, he says, "Husbands, love your wives, as Christ loved the church and gave himself up for her, … husbands should love their wives as their own bodies. He who loves his wife loves himself. … This mystery is profound, and I am saying that it refers to Christ and the church. However, let each one of you love his wife as himself" (Ephesians 5:25, 28, 32–33, ESV). In just one passage, the most quoted section on marriage, we are encouraged as men to give ourselves, love our wives as ourselves, and informed that our very marriage is the profound mystery of Christ and His love for the church.

I left out various parts of this famous passage because we as men have a tendency to read such passages and pay attention to the verses about our wives, as if to justify where we are and even excuse what we are called to do. Did you get this book to feel good or to hear God's Word for your marriage? If all I do is write things for the purpose of you having a nice casual read, you will not be walking away with anything. Instead, we have to take ownership of what Adam left open in the garden and step out in the way Jesus did for His bride.

Jesus has called you and me to be the head of the household in exactly the same way that He is head of the church. "The husband provides leadership to his wife the way Christ does to his church, not by domineering but by cherish-ing" (Ephesians 5:22–23, THE MESSAGE). In my home, I am the spiritual leader. I don't have to try to be; I don't hope to be. The Scriptures say I am, whether I like it or not. And that means that I am leading my family in a certain direc-tion, whether good or bad. Our influences and examples—to our children and grandchildren, on down the line—will last for a lifetime. For all we think we stand for, it is time we rise up and take the task of being the men God has called us to be. Notice, He also says "not by domineering but by cherishing."

As men, God made us the hunters, naturally stronger with more aggression. Most men are set on accomplishing tasks (like naming all those animals in the garden), and more often than not, physically by whatever means it takes. Yet here, right in the midst of God establishing our position, our call to leadership, our call to headship, to oversee this woman and family entrusted to us, God knew it was necessary to add "not by domineering but by cherishing." He gives us our title, and then the punch line on how to accomplish it—in love. Not as tyrants, not as brutes, not with strength, but in love, with care, and for her benefit.

See, we are so programmed to do everything in such a physical sense, we often miss that God brought us together in a holy covenant, that He is still pastoring over us, and that the Scriptures we are reading today can still speak to us.

For you as a man, you may have all kinds of ways to win her over, ask for forgiveness, become the best husband you can be, but have you stepped up to lead by doing it God's way? Jesus said that He did what He saw His Father doing, meaning He could see what God wanted Him to do and He did it (John 5:19). We too can read and see what God wants us to do—and do it. God's good like that.

Paul started off by saying:

Husbands, love your wives, as Christ loved the church and gave himself up for her, that he might sanctify her, having cleansed her by the washing of water with the word, so that he might present the church to himself in splendor, without spot or wrinkle or any such thing, that she might be holy and without blemish. In the same way husbands should love their wives as their own bodies. He who loves his wife loves himself. For no one ever hated his own flesh, but nourishes and cherishes it, just as Christ does the church, because we are members of his body.

Ephesians 5:25–30, ESV

He says, "love your wives, as Christ loved the church and gave himself up for her." He took the incentive. While the world says, "forget it and move on," He did what was right. We often overlook that Jesus took on the form of a man and had to walk in faith, just as we do. Faith is trusting what God says over everything else. Trusting in faith, He stepped out, knowing and believing "that he might sanctify her, having cleansed her by the washing of water of the word

… so that he might present the church to himself." He believed the promise, stepped into the purpose, and allowed a door for the outcome to form. We serve a God of promises. He's calling us to trust as He speaks His Word over our marriages, over our spouses in love, over our futures according to His will.

You may not be on best terms yet, even while reading this book. Some couples may even be separated, but as the man, you need to know that everything you do right now is leading your wife somewhere. She's watching you, waiting for you, thinking about you, or trying not to. Even if she has said that it's over, wants to give in, and is ready to move on, she is still aware of you, what you're doing, if only to make herself sure of your failures. God says we are to love her by giving ourselves, by the washing of the water of the word, "not by domineering but by cherishing."

We started this chapter by talking about a house divided and how such a house won't stand. You may have some things that are making your house shaky, without stability, and quite frankly as though in the midst of an earthquake. We don't understand exactly what took place in the garden of Eden, but we do know Adam was there and had a job to cover and share God's truth, His Word, with Eve. Could he have covered her more? Would the outcome have been different? I don't know, and it doesn't matter. What we do know is what God has called us to do.

Men are called to lead—don't we remind our wives of this constantly? Well men, now it is time to actually lead, and do so regardless of whether or not she is following.

You and I are the "head of the wife even as Christ is the head of the church" (Ephesians 5:23, ESV). And today, just as Christ did and just as I am striving to do, let's commit to this task. For some of you, the problem may be that you have not wanted to do this God's way, have not felt called to lead, may even feel the pressure of this role. I understand and so does God. Yet, He still thinks you, as you follow His plan, are the perfect man to lead your home.

Believe me, God is not the one who has it wrong.

As we give of ourselves today, we must note that in order to wash our wives in the water of the Word, we must know the Word ourselves, a thing which today is often reserved for Sunday mornings and children's nursery songs. I hope you don't take this lightly, because had they trusted God's Word in the garden, we would have missed out on this whole cursed world we were born into, and even of the very struggles we face in our own homes and hearts today.

Jesus said that man doesn't live on bread alone, but by the Word of God (see Matthew 4:4). As we live to keep our homes from being divided, let's unite it and ground it, first and foremost, in God's Word.

I want to encourage you today: this may seem like a big challenge if you are not a couple who prays, reads, and seeks God together. For me as a man, as I started praying over my wife, asking in prayer, sharing God's Word, speaking promises over our marriage, and always pointing back to what God has written for us, our home began to grow and change. And if you are still here trying to fine-tune your wife into the woman you've always dreamed of, please, don't be deceived. Your job is to help your heavenly Father as He shapes her, by way of His love and your expression of it. He calls us to love and wash her in the Word "so that he might present the church to himself in splendor, without spot or wrinkle or any such thing, that she might be holy and without blemish."

Get to know the Word, start praying it, speaking it, believing it, and living it!

> "So shall my word be that goes out from my mouth; it shall not return to me empty, but it shall accomplish that which I purpose, and shall succeed in the thing for which I sent it."
>
> *Isaiah 55:11, ESV*

DAY 9: HER PART

So, we gave your husband a good telling off, put him in his place, or directed him rather. Believe me, I have heard it from women so many times: "If he would just lead;" "He's the one who is the spiritual leader;" "Why doesn't he do what he's called to do?" It's true—he is to lead like his life depends upon it. We just heard from God on this. So where does this leave you? A puppet? A slave? Someone who is second? Not at all, but it does mean that as he is called to lead, you are called to follow.

It was just a few years ago while driving that I heard this song on the airwaves:

"Lead me with strong hands

Stand up when I can't

Don't leave me hungry for love

Chasing dreams, but what about us?

Show me you're willing to fight

That I'm still the love of your life

I know we call this our home

But I still feel alone."[1]

In tears while driving, I heard the call to stand up, to lead better. God brought to my remembrance so many Scriptures, encouraging me to depend on my God even more. But where is my wife in this? Yes, she is the one crying out for more of me, but what is often overlooked in this song is the fact that she is submitted in her saying "lead me."

---

[1] Sanctus Real. "Lead Me." *Pieces of a Real Heart*. Sparrow Records, 2010.

She isn't saying do as I say, but do as God has called, and ladies, let me help you out. Having a husband encouraged to lead is better than a bitter one who is forced to lead. It's the same as having a wife who is choosing to submit as opposed to being told to be "subject" to. I know this sounds like I'm mixing words, but there is a big difference between my wife choosing to submit and my telling her to be subject to what I say.

You see, just as I charged your husband to get after leading, covering, and protecting you, which he should choose to do, I am also asking you today, are you able to say "lead me" and walk with him as he does so? Are you able to say, "I may disagree on some of the directions you take, but I am choosing in faith to follow"? Am I saying follow him into sin and do things that are out of God's will? No! But I am saying that he is going to have a path he feels he should walk on, and the first person he needs alongside of him is you. As I sit here writing this, my wife is in the same room while my kids watch the Red Sox hopefully win the 2013 World Series. In my life, the reason I am able to be a better Christian, husband, and father, write this book, travel, speak, and go on to accomplish all I can is because of my wife and helper. She chooses to come alongside me, believing that the first call on her life is to be my other half while giving all of herself.

Biblically, theologically, why would God call a woman in this day and age, who is under the New Covenant, to submit? Well, in Genesis, even before the curse, she was made his helper; and since our separation from God's presence in the garden, it is now in her nature, the flesh, to be in opposition to doing so. I did say this chapter was about "her part," so:

> To the woman he said, "I will surely multiply your pain in childbearing; in
> pain you shall bring forth children. Your desire shall be for your husband,
> and he shall rule over you."
>
> *Genesis 3:16, ESV*

Upon reading this, people might say we are no longer under the curse. Though it's true for us in spirit, our flesh still is. Do you know any woman, Christian or not, who doesn't have pain in childbearing? Or a man who doesn't have to work hard to provide? I was present at all my children's births, and I got to witness firsthand just how tough my wife is. AMEN!

God said, "Your desire shall be for your husband, and he shall rule over you." Some translations even go so far as to say, "And you will desire to control your husband, but he will rule over you" (NLT). Whichever translation we look at, we have to see that the way God laid this out is for the wife's focus to be on her husband. At times she might be telling him which way to turn at the light or pointing out that his shoes never seem to find a place; but a woman who loves God and loves her husband simply wants to come alongside to help accomplish the vision God has given to them as one.

So what is the woman's role? We saw in day 8 that Paul challenged the men, as the head, to wash their wives in the Word. In that same passage, Paul's first personal direction to women is this: "submit to your own husbands, as to the Lord" (Ephesians 5:22, ESV). Submit as to the Lord? Yes, God calls the wife to have that same kind of childlike faith, the kind that caused her to trust in Jesus as her Lord and Savior, in believing her submission will be blessed as she helps her husband in his call to lead.

Some years ago I wrote about a newly formed website that promoted having affairs. With millions and millions of subscribers and members, their site helped set up people to find one another in order to cheat on their spouses and break their covenant of marriage. As I posted my blog, I was surprised to see an almost instant response from the very website, saying, "liberating women from Ephesians 5:22." Not only was this website blatantly sinful, but it was also boasting about its agenda, its rebellion to God's Word. This fact alone is a good enough reason to stop and consider, how does a woman's "choosing" to submit not only honor and support her husband, but honor her God? If an affair represents rebellion in its highest form, then wouldn't it make sense that by a woman choosing to submit in the smaller things, she would have conditioned herself against ever having an affair?

We protect our marriages by being aware of such patterns. I'm getting real here, because sadly, I see so many affairs even within the church today. Remember that people are within the church walls, but only true Christians are in Christ. Judas probably heard Jesus' messages and would have known every beat and rhythm to all of the worship songs, but was he in Christ? Did he abide in Him?

You see, when Paul writes, "submit to your own husband, as to the Lord," that's exactly where you need to start. If you view your submission to your husband as to *him*, first and foremost, then when times get challenging, you will be more likely to rebel. But if you begin with your choosing to submit as to the Lord, and in the same way he is choosing to lead the household as to the Lord, the picture starts to make sense.

It is now that the start of Ephesians 5:21 (ESV) should be fully understood, "… submitting to one another out of reverence for Christ." My leading, and my wife's following isn't about us personally, but about Jesus, and we are blessed to reap the benefits.

> For the husband is the head of the wife even as Christ is the head of the church, his body, and is himself its Savior. Now as the church submits to Christ, so also wives should submit in everything to their husbands.
>
> *Ephesians 5:23–24*

As I lead my wife, give myself for her, cover and wash her in the Word, she receives, says yes, and hears what I say when Satan enters the garden—when I am concerned about finances, when I have a heavy heart and need my best friend to come alongside, help me, and trust God with me. If not, just as it was bad that man was alone in the garden, I will feel just as alone in the marriage, because instead of unity, there will be division against all I am trying to lead my family into.

It's important to add here that many men don't know how to lead, so as they are learning and starting to take steps, the last thing they need is a wife who is trying to lead. Why did Adam follow Eve in the eating of the fruit? Was she more dominant, or was he unable to lead?

And just as many women are not going to be comfortable submitting, possibly never seeing it modeled by another woman, the husband is going to have to be aware that this will take time by the sowing of seeds, by mutual submission to God, believing for a harvest as the roles develop.

Women, you are going to naturally be bent toward only wanting to submit to the things you agree with, but that is not submission. That's agreement. It will feel uncomfortable for the flesh, even frustrating, causing you to want to state your case and explain your perspective. It's great to talk and hear out both sides, but you have to believe that the God who made you and has blessed your marriage will be leading your husband, just as your husband is called to lead your home.

As this all starts to form and shape, you will be surprised how smooth it can make your marriage. It isn't always going to be, but when it does flow, it's beautiful. I have a responsibility to lead, I know, but that doesn't mean I don't ask my wife to be equally involved in all of our planning. As a man, spouse, and father, why wouldn't I want her, who is my other half, to give her opinions and ideas, striving to help us make the right choices?

As the spiritual leader, I was the one who felt called to structure when we pray, read, have Bible studies with the kids, worship, attend church, and so on, but my wife was right there hearing me out and giving suggestions. We made those decisions together.

If she is in rebellion to all of this, how can we have a peaceful home? But when my kids see me submitting to Christ, who is head of the church, and see my wife likewise submitted to me trying to lead the home, there is peace.

It is sad but not surprising that most family shows on television always have the dad as some buffoon that the mother hardly listens to. The world has thumbed its sinful nose at God's ways because a balanced relationship is a huge blessing.

If you entered our home today, I'd tell you that I was the one thinking about the cost we paid many years ago, all about the location, and how long we may live here; but she was involved in all of those conversations.

As you enter our doors and see the four different kinds of wallpaper on our walls, the style of furniture, which room she homeschools in, this is all my wife's doing, but she wanted to hear my opinions every step of the way. Why? Because I am aware of our budget, and as her covering, I have to run it through the plan for the future for our family.

When we made the choice to have three kids, knowing she would need a bigger car, did I simply go out and buy whatever I thought she should have and bring it home, as if she wouldn't have a preference as she taxis the mini humans all about town? Of course not.

As a couple, you will learn how you best work together, you will learn to hear each other out, look to identify your partner's preferences, and find one another's rhythms.

What I am saying, ladies, is your submission isn't about giving up who you are and becoming a robot. It's about supporting your husband as he strives to lead. The two of you have your own special roles, and this is the way God designed it to work.

I encourage the two of you to read the end of Ephesians 5 as it flows into Ephesians 6. You will notice how God tells wives to submit to their husbands, then tells children to obey their parents, and finally tells how slaves should obey their masters. These three statements are consistent in thought. Yes, there is a mutual submission to God in our individual roles, but ladies, God's plan is for you to show the family how to support and build up your husband, through submission, as he covers and leads.

DAY 10: LOVE YOUR WIFE AS YOURSELF

At times, I think I must have had God shaking His head many, many times. How He didn't call down burning sulfur, boils, and plagues upon me, I do not know. Our first year or so together, of romance, passion, and on into pregnancy, was amazing. But as my wife's emotions turned from me to our son within her womb, I was gradually getting less attention and wasn't as secure in our future. So not knowing the Lord, I gradually began to think more and more about myself. But once she gave birth to Dakota, we were joyous over our baby boy's arrival, and I had adjusted to not being the center of her attention.

Eventually, her body gradually transformed from an incubator back into that of a woman, and her focus was back toward us. By this time, I had learned to live each day (though not contentedly) with our focus on the baby, and not as much on one another.

One of the things this showed me was that I loved her giving me attention, and that I needed to feel loved. This being true of all right-minded men, look at the result it had on me. Even though I was motivated and rose up to the task, it caused me to dwell a lot on myself. Then when she had given birth and was back to needing my attention, I had adjusted to simply maintaining.

God does not want you to have a relationship that is simply maintaining, but one where each person is always giving his or her all.

Had I known this then, and had I known Ephesians 5:25 (esv), "Husbands, love your wives, as Christ loved the church and gave himself up for her," I would have instead focused more on giving her the affection she needed, and as her hormones were changing back, she would not have felt a difference.

See, my standard wasn't how much my wife loved me, but how much I myself needed to be loved.

Christ came to save us because He wanted us as part of His life, so much so that out of that love He gave His very best. We are told that Jesus, "for the joy set before him he endured the cross" (Hebrews 12:2).

Years later, after we had come to faith, my wife said she wanted one or two more children. These pregnancies were very different. I knew going into them that I was going to love my wife as I love myself, as Christ loved the church. I viewed this as a great privilege, one in which I was able to die to self even more by pouring myself out.

Having this mindset in my marriage means that the same way I want to be loved, whether things are good or bad, is the way I need to love my wife.

Paul then compares our loving our wives as our own bodies to how "Christ does the church, because we are members of his body" (Ephesians 5:29–30, ESV).

Because He is the head of the church and because He needs His body to function smoothly in order for the Gospel to keep going out across the world, He continues to pour His love out upon us each day. Thank You, Lord! What a privilege to be His body, the body of Christ.

Paul even says, "For no one ever hated his own flesh, but nourishes and cherishes it, just as Christ does the church" (Ephesians 5:29, ESV).

We often sit back expecting our wives to meet us where we are, but because we are to lead, we need to lead in pouring out our love. If you can't put this into practice, she will feel it. And just like my wife, five months after giving birth, when she needed my affirmation the most, she was getting a less-than-godly standard of love. As a man, why would I want to love anyone less than the standard by which I want to be loved, and less than the standard by which "Christ loved the church and gave himself up for her" (Ephesians 5:25, ESV)?

I wanted to take more time today for your personal consideration and discussion. We see over and over in the Bible situations in which women don't feel loved. Yet, we see Jesus stand up for them, ready to forgive their sins and confirm His love.

Had He not, would we have seen how loving He really is? Consider this: when things get bad, what would happen if we didn't have His Word to encourage us, to remind us we are loved and that we are the object of His affection? Could we make it through each day?

When we talk about running the race of life and living for Christ, we can say this because we know He is for us, encouraging us, and will be at the end to welcome us into His presence. Your wife, here and now, despite what she may say, also needs to be affirmed by you. She is constantly being bombarded by the world every day to get her approval from everything else. Is she the right weight, size, and shape? Does she parent right; is she a good spouse; is she making the right choices?

As you start loving and affirming her, she will find her identity more in being your spouse than by what she is hearing and seeing every day. Just as we talked about you washing her in the Word, you also need to love and affirm her.

Tonight, I would like the two of you to open up for a time of discussion. Pray beforehand that there would be peace, that the Holy Spirit would lead, and that the time would be used to draw you closer. Be aware of getting defensive or trying to point the finger. This is simply so you can begin to be more open and to learn how as a husband you can better love your wife. This isn't a time for your wife to call you out, but a time of bonding, maybe breaking down, and then rebuilding. Discuss these verses:

1. "He who finds a wife finds a good thing" (Proverbs 18:22, ESV); "her husband … praises her" (Proverbs 31:28).

How do I as a man live up to speaking life and affirmation over my wife? Is it easy for me to give compliments, to encourage, and look to the good that she does?

2. "You are altogether beautiful, my love; there is no flaw in you" (Song of Solomon 4:7, ESV).

How do I as a man cherish my wife above other women, affirming her beauty, looking to the positive, and live understanding that this is God's standard of beauty for me?

3. "Husbands, love your wives, as Christ loved the church and gave himself up for her" (Ephesians 5:25).

How do I put my walk, wife, and family before my needs and myself? I am not saying to say "how high" when your wife says, "jump," as that, in and of itself, can be dangerous. What I am saying is how do you love her in a way that invites her to walk alongside you, knowing that you have her best interests at heart?

If a wife feels unloved, it is not an excuse for her to sin or depart from the faith, as our first priority is always with God. But as you build this relationship and give time and focus to nurture it, your love and affirmation will help her to blossom.

DAY 11: RESPECT YOUR HUSBAND

However, let each one of you love his wife as himself, and let the wife see that she respects her husband.

Ephesians 5:33, ESV

Amazingly, both the man and the wife are addressed in the same passage. The man, "you," is called to love; and the "wife" is immediately called to respect "her husband."

Is this hard to do? Will you do it only if he deserves it? Do you feel like you respect him in certain things but not others? There are so many opinions on this idea and that's the reason why books have been written on the subject of respect. Why is it so important? Shouldn't I as a man also live to honor and respect my wife? So why has this been such a hot topic for women?

In a nutshell, it's obvious. When God spoke in the garden, when He gave His directions, who spoke up against and paved a road for others to do so? It was Satan, the "father of lies," who first disrespected God and went his own way. It was Satan who laid the groundwork for rebellion and opposition to God's plans.

So God leads and oversees, Jesus leads and oversees, and man leads and oversees. Therefore, the first person who needs to show respect for her husband is his wife. If the man is to lead his family by respecting God, then his wife, as she helps lead the children and as she lives of life of bearing witness to others, does so in her respecting her husband.

How am I to lead my children if the direction, plan, and vision for our family is contested by my wife? If, when I am speaking, my wife mocks me, doesn't listen, doesn't abide by what I say, or approve of my decisions, how will my kids see my position and look to it as authoritative? Consider now that I am already stepping into the role of submitting to Christ, loving my wife, leading her, while also encouraging her to come alongside me in our future as my greatest help, prayer warrior, and even critic.

Wives, I have to tell you that your position on this will absolutely have prolonged effects on both yours and your husband's lives. I have seen situations where men had so much respect and a platform of influence until their wives came around, then they were dissected and mocked. This isn't always an attack on the man either; this can simply be the way the spouse chooses to carry herself.

A few years back, I watched Billy Graham's "My Hope America" on television. He was a great man, and the Lord used him and his life in pursuit of God. Yet, it was very satisfying to hear his grandson on a live newscast say, "Let's not forgot my grandmother. Without her, he couldn't have done the things he did." How right he is! As a young couple, they discussed what God had called Billy to do, and his wife understood and was in agreement. Imagine if, while he travelled, she chose not to do her part as a mother. When they agreed on her role while he was away, she kept to it: the home, the reading, praying, schooling, and so on. Billy couldn't be qualified for ministry if his home wasn't in order; so his wife was just as much a part of his outreach as he was. Their legacy together, in their submission to Christ, is lived on in their children and grandchildren. Fruit has been borne from their labor. There is reaping from their sowing.

With three children, a house, bills, clothes, and responsibilities, how can I possibly expect to fulfill the call on my life if there is no one to help me? We are told that, "He who finds a wife finds a good thing" (Proverbs 18:22, ESV). "She does him good, and not harm, all the days of her life" (Proverbs 31:12, ESV). Even more so, a verse that we hold close and dear is 1 Corinthians 11:7, "woman is the glory of man."

Society has fooled women into thinking that unless she is up front and making the big decisions that she is second-class or of lower stature. But in God's eyes, as I try to work out my salvation with fear and trembling and as I try to lead both my wife and my family, she is the first person to give support and approval to my path because she is also tied to it. Just as God didn't tell me to try to be the head, but said, "the husband *is* the head of the wife," she is also to "respect."

Disclaimer: Your husband will not always make the best decisions; so if you are waiting for him to be "super husband" and have everything together before you respect him, know that he is at a disability because you are not by his side supporting him on this path. If he feels he has to work for your respect, which isn't biblical, it will hinder his ability to lead.

Tracy and I strived to make our marriage work long before we knew the Lord. And of all the times I felt defeated or crushed, there was none more than when I was disrespected. If there is one thing I can tell you about men, about anger, about stepping back from a relationship, and about wanting out, it has typically come from a place of being disrespected.

Just as God told him he would work "by the sweat of [his] face" (Genesis 3:19, ESV) to provide, within each man is a desire to succeed, to do a good job, and to "be the man." As cheesy as it sounds, that is built into the inner parts of your husband, and just as you thrive best when you are feeling loved, your husband will also thrive most when he is being respected.

As we had an open discussion in the last chapter, tonight we need to do more of the same. I understand that even in these circumstances, things can get uncomfortable and things can seem confrontational. We have to work through those things with love and maturity so we can be open with one another and provide a safe place to share and rebuild.

She does him good, and not harm, all the days of her life.

Proverbs 31:12, ESV

1. How do you as a wife, out of respect for God and your husband, live in a way that is respectful and supportive of the person God has called him to be?

It is better to live in a desert land than with a quarrelsome and fretful woman.

Proverbs 21:19, ESV

2. As his helper, spouse, and possibly mother of his children, in what ways can you learn to walk alongside him to strengthen him and encourage him, rather than stepping in to question and challenge? Are you content knowing that God's grace is upon you to support him and speak life, even when you don't always agree?

Many women do noble things, but you surpass them all.

Proverbs 31:29

3. Aside from your husband, God has called you to live a noble life, one that seeks after righteousness and holiness. Jesus Christ makes us righteous and holy, but others only see it through our interactions. In a practical sense, how can you show your husband your respect for him in the daily interactions? Listening, making time, and/or going out of your way?

DAY 12: WHY CAN'T WE BE FRIENDS? [1]

If you listen to what people are talking about and look at what's encouraging them or discouraging them, so much of it is grounded in friendship. You might hear someone advise a friend to cut people out of their lives who prove to be bad friends or getting advice and comfort from people who are "true" friends, "good" friends, or even "best" friends. As a form of endearment we may even tell someone, "I consider you a true friend."

Yet why, in marriage today, is friendship rarely ever considered? The Hollywood movies rarely have the lead character end up with the best friend, but instead with someone who makes them breathless and holds their attention, someone they can't get enough of.

Friendship is something we encounter as a child, entering school for the first time. We feel more confident when we make friends and less confident when we don't. When we get into our teens and into high school, we have best friends, people in whom we confide and share our struggles, who are there for us along the way.

On into adulthood, we have those friends from childhood or the ones who have walked through some hard seasons with whom we will be friends until we die.

All of this is as it should be, the way it's meant to be. Even God Himself is in friendship, by His nature, as God the Father, God the Son, and God the Holy Spirit—the Holy Trinity. And because we are made in God's image, is there any other way we should expect to interact with people, other than through friendship, as we open ourselves up to love people?

Why then, within our marriages, the most sacred union with another person, is friendship so rarely focused on and pursued? We feel we need people

[1] War. "Why Can't We Be Friends?" *Why Can't We Be Friends?* United Artists Records, 1975.

around us that we can open up with, share our deepest thoughts and fears with, even more so than our spouse. Is there any wonder why we can often feel so distant from our spouse?

This should not be; our very best friend should be our spouse. As we read through the pages of Scripture, the first union between two humans was of companionship, relationship, marriage, and friendship. They were put together for one another, and that plan has not changed. If we were to ask the wisest man if it is important for a man and woman to be friends in marriage, I have no doubt that he would point us to the Shulamite woman's words in Song of Solomon 5:16, "This is my beloved and this is my friend, O daughters of Jerusalem" (ESV). Her beloved, her friend. The one she has been getting to know, thinking nonstop about and distracted by. Her spouse!

It's been years since I lived in Liverpool, but recently, an old friend messaged me through Facebook. After many years of marriage, he told me he and his wife had decided to call it quits. They had mutually agreed to learn how to get along, for the sake of the kids, so their children could still have the kind of life they deserve.

The main reason for the split, he wrote, was because though they still "cared" for each other, they had fallen "out of love." Not being believers and having no idea of what true agape love is, my suggestion to them was that they were simply experiencing what so many couples do. After the first few years and all the passion and romance, dating, and bonding, they took inventory and realized they had become two humans living together, bonded by marriage, but no longer enjoying one another or making the time or effort to do so.

The reason they got married in the first place was because they had formed a relationship by "relating," and that this bond, this time spent together, this effort to see one another, enjoy one another, hear one another out, consider one another, and go out of their way for one another created a thriving friendship. At the core it was handled with care as something that mattered to them both. And it's through this lens that we have the greatest of friendships, and more importantly, a friendship with our spouse.

I love the picture of how Adam walked with God in the garden. He spent time with Him, was able to ask Him anything, gaze upon His presence, simply enjoying who God was as His friend.

But as time went on and sin took hold, Adam and Eve considered good and evil, weighed the options, and when God came looking again for Adam to spend time with him, Adam hid, backed off, wasn't available for the confident and God-centered friendship he had enjoyed.

This is what happens when we allow the focus in our marriage to get off center. When we stop spending quality time with one another, stop going the extra mile, and stop thinking in favor of our spouse, we too will not experience the friendship we once enjoyed.

Adam was close with God, but then he became distant. Do you remember when you first met your spouse? What drew you together; what sparked interest, and what did you see in one another that was appealing?

Part of the enjoyment in that season of pursuit was that your friendship was growing and a relationship was being built. There is an excitement in thinking more of your spouse than yourself. Think of the joy it brought to do something sacrificial for them, knowing it would make their day.

God knows where you are in your marriage, and He still wants you to pursue both—friendship with Him and friendship with your spouse. We read in Genesis 5:24, "Enoch walked with God, and he was not, for God took him" (ESV). You can't walk with someone very long without forming a deeper friendship. For us in our marriages, our friendship will be one of the foundations that allow us to keep walking together, not hiding in the bushes, but having the confident, humble, out-in-the-open marriage we need.

When we think of the Gospel—the good news of what Jesus came to accomplish and the love He expressed—we so often focus on the cross, by which He took our sins upon Himself, or we look to His healing powers, by which He changed people's lives, or the multiplication of food or the walking on water and so on. But what sticks out, here and now for this chapter, is what He actually accomplished as He was doing all of these things.

Before He came to die, resurrect, and forgive, we were at odds with Him, separate from Him, enemies of God, still hiding in the bushes. But what was His overall goal? What was the focus of His love? "Greater love has no one than this, that someone lay down his life for his friends" (John 15:13, ESV). Think about that! The greatest expression of love was to lay down His life for His FRIENDS. WOW! To take us from hiding behind the bushes, to tear down the veil that separates us from God, to bring us back into unity, on the same page, with open love.

Let me ask you: Where are you two as a couple today? Are you open; is there unity; are you willing to make the effort for your spouse, to be the person they need, and who God made you to be?

Jesus went on to say, "You are my friends if you do what I command you. No longer do I call you servants, for the servant does not know what his master is doing; but I have called you friends ..." (John 15:14–15, ESV).

You have been going strong these first twelve chapters, getting deep into the ins-and-outs of God's Word and the core truths that will hold us together, convict us in love, and lay a foundation for what's ahead. Tonight, why not take some time to pray and to think back to what you first did when you were together. Some of the pictures you may have taken; messages you sent; plans you talked about; sacrifices you made. Why not plan ahead and schedule a regular date night, a time to pursue one another, relate, and stir up some of what may be lacking in your friendship?

DAY 13: IN YOUR ANGER, DO NOT SIN!

At our church, we have an outreach called "Young Lives." The goal is to have men who have families and are raising children sit with younger, recently new fathers to encourage and sow into them. Last night, one question came up, "How do we, as men, deal with our anger?"

The young man asking the question described his situation. He had pulled into his driveway and clipped his car against the wall. As he heard the crunch and pictured the damage, in anger, he jumped out of his car and ran into the house. He confessed that, upon entering his home, he held and cuddled his newborn daughter for comfort and a feeling of satisfaction while at the same time yelling at his wife to be quiet. As he took out all of his frustration on her, he knew it was wrong. He felt bad about it, yet he went full steam ahead with no idea how to handle it.

As I think back on the early years of my marriage, I remember getting to a point where I gave and gave and gave, feeling absolutely spent and like I was getting nothing in return. Our son, Dakota, was around six months old, and after feeling like I had bent over backwards trying to be "super husband," but not addressing certain things along the way, I remember getting into it with my wife and just straight saying to myself "f this."

I had taken enough, felt like I had no voice, had blown my fuse, and didn't know what to do. This was BC ("Before Christ"), by the way, so that kind of language was the norm, sadly.

But from then on, any time I was challenged, didn't feel loved, or felt disrespected, I would say whatever was on my mind. Things I would never have imagined saying to my Tracy I said, and soon, things escalated.

We began arguing, fighting, name calling, giving the silent treatment, taking off for a drive, blasting each other viciously, and so on. We didn't know what was happening, and we didn't know how to slow things down.

Keep in mind that I grew up in Liverpool, a culture where it was the norm to get into altercations daily. There could be a shouting match or you might have to act puffed up to avoid a fight. Or there may be something going down where you have to gauge the situation, which normally meant swearing at whomever was standing in your way and saying a mixture of things to try to intimidate them to see if they were for real.

I was raised with the mindset that using your voice and body language was a defense mechanism to ward off trouble. But now, just like when I was pushed to the edge on the street, as I was being pushed into a corner in my marriage, I was taking out my wrath on my beautiful wife. Not that she was innocent; it does take two. But that is not any sort of an excuse for my actions or yours.

As our fights grew and grew, my fists went into walls, the names called were absolutely degrading, and almost anything that came to my mind was spouted out.

I began to see the extent of just how angry I could get and how, like so many, I couldn't control myself and didn't know how to rightly vent.

How could a guy from England, bred this way (we could say), possibly begin to exercise any of the characteristics of love spoken about in 1 Corinthians 13?

In the next few chapters, I want to spend time looking at these specific characteristics, the ones found in the very verses Tracy and I heard the night we wed in Vegas. As we do, hopefully you will see the struggles within yourself, the struggles with anger you may have and how to embrace the change.

> Love is patient, love is kind. It does not envy, it does not boast, it is not proud. It does not dishonor others, it is not self-seeking, it is not easily angered, it keeps no record of wrongs. Love does not delight in evil but rejoices with the truth. It always protects, always trusts, always hopes, always perseveres. Love never fails.
>
> *1 Corinthians 13:4–8*

Reading over this passage, I can say with absolute confidence that I have blown all that Paul lists here as my anger grew and grew and got the best of me. It felt comfortable clenching my fists, grinding my teeth, speaking more intensely, and feeling I had to get my point across.

As our marriage got worse and we were by now throwing divorce at each other like it was no big deal, I remember my wife getting into her car as she was about to leave. As she did, I ran out to the garage, undoubtedly to shout some rude remark, to which she slammed the door in my face. The door connected with my leg full force. Whether she intended it or not, I felt disrespected again, belittled, and here was my wife leaving our home because of our anger.

What could I do? What would you do? What did that young man do after the car hit the wall? I did what I had learned to do—blasted the garage door open, ran up to the car, and as she was leaving, I smashed my fist down on the windshield as hard as possible. It cracked the windshield, and as she got out of the car in shock, the noise (and her mother coming over) resulted in the police being called, and I was in trouble. Although we were not physical, I look back now as that time as life changing.

This was definitely one of the events God used to get my attention, as it ended with my having to take anger management classes for several weeks.

It was a huge wake-up call for my wife and for me, but it was also something that would become useful to me for the rest of my life.

In those classes I learned that anger is an emotion—one we are born with and that is triggered based on the situations we encounter. Just as on the streets of Liverpool, when fear or offense came, anger would rise up and set the tone for what I would choose to do next.

With my marriage, all the conflicts I hadn't addressed had pushed me into a corner, and I couldn't take it anymore. Anger was the emotion, the red flag, saying this is too much, but it wasn't the anger that was the problem. It was how I reacted when I was angry. How my wife slammed the door when she was angry, or even, for better understanding, how the young man mentioned in the beginning of this chapter, after hitting the wall, was able to react to his daughter in love yet reacted another way to his wife while being angry the whole time. This is your issue with anger too—how you react.

It's with this understanding that we see the Scriptures in the Bible ring true: "Be angry and do not sin; do not let the sun go down on your anger, and give no opportunity to the devil" (Ephesians 4:26–27, ESV).

So this emotion is a part of our human nature. It's a trigger that should cause us to think even more about whatever the situation may be. But anger isn't necessarily sin because Jesus got angry. In the gospel of Mark, we read the story of Jesus healing a man with a deformed hand, but because it was the

Sabbath, the Pharisees got mad. As Jesus asked them a question, one which they didn't answer, we are told that Jesus "looked around at them with anger [and] grieved at their hardness of heart" (Mark 3:5, ESV). He looked at them with anger. He was angry, got upset, had a problem; yet the Bible says He never sinned, ever. What He did next, even though He was angry, was to simply tell the man to stretch out his hand and He healed him. He was angry but didn't sin. But I did. I wasn't patient, wasn't kind; I was self-seeking and lacking love.

Everyone gets angry, women just as much. It's just that typically men react more with shouting and more easily get to the point of being physical. We shout much louder, are generally stronger, and can be a lot more imposing. God even refers to the woman as the weaker partner or vessel (1 Peter 3:7).

If that verse offends you, think about it. How many times do you see an altercation in the street or witness someone come to the house to start a fight and the wife rolls up her sleeves, expected to handle business? You don't; it's generally men who throw fists. Society has also bred aggression into men, often-times as something to be glorified. So please, don't use this chapter as a way for you, wife, to guilt-trip your husband. I can tell you, he feels guilt, knows it's wrong, and that there is a better way to handle things. Of all the times we have fought, shouted, took off, and gone overboard, I always knew I would regret it and that I was doing nothing positive for our marriage. In my anger and moments of despair, I was falling into sin.

That night at Young Lives, as we were seated before these young fathers, I let them know the reality of the situations they were in. Fights may start with shouting, escalating to throwing and smashing things, even to pointing in one another's face, then pushing and shoving, grabbing ahold of, and then, who knows? Being physical, even to the point of jail time? They needed to know this because statistics show this. They needed to know this because it's reality. I know what it's like to be pushed into a corner, and when our voices aren't heard or our needs aren't being met, this is how we can react in our anger. They needed to know this just as much as you need to know this. Infidelity destroys many a marriage but so does anger. Everything that was promised is tossed aside, and we say "uncle," leading to the way of wrath.

However, there is hope and there is grace as we trust in God's Word and listen to His Holy Spirit for direction. Because we are believers and because love never fails, we should be able to bear the fruit of what's inside of us—the fruit of the Holy Spirit.

But the fruit of the Spirit is love … gentleness and self-control.

Galatians 5:22–23

Just because you are still together doesn't mean that inside, one of you isn't going through hell dealing with it or the results.

We told that young man that night what he should have done. Rather than going into the house fully knowing he was angry, he should have gone for a walk, called a friend, got some prayer, and thought about the situation. I am convinced that, had he done that, he would have been strengthened by God Almighty to love both his daughter and his wife. He would have heard that still small voice saying, "I am counting on you to love My daughter, your wife."

Below are some verses that speak clearly about how we should react when dealing with our anger. I learned to recognize how I am feeling, even when things are frustrating and I feel my back is up against the wall. When things get dark, I need to shine some light, God's Word, into the situation. I remind myself of what He says, consider my role as the head of the home, and remember that love never fails.

Just as much as I learned to deal with my anger, my wife also had to recognize when she gets angry. Our interactions can play a definite part in pushing one another's buttons.

This is not a "Pass Go" card for women to do anything they want to control their spouse if he gets angry. This is a call for both of you, women included, to gauge your anger, consider how you react, and be mature.

I have seen just as many women refuse to speak, go off into serious sin, or be manipulative in situations, knowing they can use his shortcomings against him.

We need love! We need to be open to discuss and pray about these things, without accusing and judging.

May these verses speak to you and your spouse, as they have to Tracy and me. We have discussed them many times, and I encourage you and your spouse to do the same.

Husbands, love your wives, and do not be harsh with them.

Colossians 3:19, ESV

Likewise, husbands, live with your wives in an understanding way, showing honor to the woman as the weaker vessel …

1 Peter 3:7, ESV

DAY 14: STILL ANGRY? SPEAK LIFE!

As we tackled anger in the more physical sense in the prior chapter, we talked about how it stems from our being pushed into a corner, feeling we have to defend ourselves and that we don't have anyone on our side. As a couple, with God at the center, knowing we are now united in a covenant and have our spouse at our side, we need to expose one of the most dangerous weapons at work to destroy our homes every day. Can you take a guess at what it is?

American culture is founded on freedom. One of these freedoms is "freedom of speech." We are bred thinking everything we feel should be expressed and hide behind sayings as ridiculous as "I just tell it like it is." Let me help the whole world out right here, and yes, I just said that. The only way anyone "tells it like it is" is when he or she speaks God's Word because it is the only truth there is. You may tell what you feel or say what you think, but if you are going to speak truth that brings life, it must be God's Word.

Of all the holes I punched in walls or things tossed and thrown around our home, there was nothing more destructively tossed and thrown around our marriage than *our words*. Whoever said, "sticks and stones may break my bones but words will never hurt me" was in cohorts with the devil. He is "the father of lies" (John 8:44), and that little limerick is a lie from the pit of hell. Note that it was also through his words that the serpent first deceived Eve, asking her, "Did God really say …?" (Genesis 3:1).

What we say is so profound and powerful in both the positive and the negative. We need to understand our future is on the tip of our tongue.

In those years of pain and hurt, I said so many things to my wife, as did she to me, that we just didn't mean. Seeing that one of us wasn't giving our full attention to the concern at hand, or feeling we had been wronged, as the situations got more heated, we could spout out just about anything to get a reaction or to cut down. I'd challenge her parenting, her love for me, her body, what her focus was, and often it was a form of defense, saying I had had enough. She would retaliate, and together, we extended the borders of our verbal battleground even further. Soon, nothing was off limits as to what could be said.

We dug deeper and deeper into one another's souls and futures by slicing away at the foundation we had built. It's no coincidence that Solomon, the wisest man who ever lived, penned, "The tongue has the power of life and death, and those who love it will eat its fruit" (Proverbs 18:21). Literally speaking it, proclaiming it, establishing it, remembering it, over and over going around in our heads and hearts what we said or was said. We went on eating of its fruit long after it had been spoken. Was it ripening to beauty and refreshment, or was it decaying, rotten, and deadly? We need love! We need to be open to discuss and pray about these things without accusing and judging.

What you speak to one another in moments of rage will take who knows how long to heal, if ever, as you then have to believe your spouse never meant what they said to you.

Recently I heard of a couple that, almost in a boasting way, said, "When we fight, we let it all out; we go at it and make sure it's all out in the open. Then we make up, forget about it, and move on."

Crazy! Absolutely crazy! While this may sound mature in theory, we as humans have a soul, and we carry emotions. Being beaten up verbally by your spouse in any way will do your soul no good and will leave lasting scars. There is a reason the Bible says, "Too much talk leads to sin. Be sensible and keep your mouth shut" (Proverbs 10:19, NLT). Thank You, Lord! And what is it James thinks we need to know? "Know this, my beloved brothers: let every person be quick to hear, slow to speak, slow to anger" (James 1:19, ESV).

So as you feel that anger and feel the need to speak out and plead your case, put the brakes on and be aware that your spouse is going to receive what you say as coming right from your heart, "for out of the abundance of the heart [the] mouth speaks" (Luke 6:45, ESV). Sadly, in the times when you are trying to reconcile, even if you are not speaking confrontationally out of a wounded and angry heart, your spouse won't be able to receive your love as easily, because they will have learned to guard themselves against the very words you speak. "Guard your heart above all else, for it determines the course of your life" (Proverbs 4:23, NLT).

We spoke so much death and pain over one another that when we tried to reconcile, apologize, and redirect our path in love, we didn't have the trust or confidence. My wife didn't see me as her covering, her support, her protector, but instead, her problem, enemy, and the issue. I too didn't see her as my best friend, companion, partner, or in any way, my beloved helper.

Undoubtedly, you have experienced what is referred to as "loose lips, sinking ships" in your relationship. You have felt it okay to state your case, testify why you are mad, or speak it "like it is." My hope is that you both can see that there are couples all over the world with similar problems, in the same boat, working to overcome what we say to one another daily.

My wife and I fought so many times, yet we strived to catch when we had gone too far or were about to tread into deeper water as anger rose up. As we did, we were learning to take responsibility for our actions and our words.

I can blame her all day for the reasons why I said this and did that, but can I stand before God and do so?

Can she justify why she is bitter, wound up, and doing nothing to help me because I was unloving?

With God on our side, "nothing will be impossible" (Luke 1:37, ESV), but we have to walk in that, trusting Him. What we did was make a statement, a sentence that we both believed and would strive to live for. This was part of our promise to one another, in that we could recite this sentence and be reminded of our love, hopes, and promises.

"Let's not do this; this isn't God's best; we love one another."

And that was that. Something simple that could be said or remembered in an instant.

We began to speak it and remind one another of it. At certain times, things can get heated; but this one sentence is our reminder, along with (and second to) God's Word.

Why not spend some time right now reading the following passage of Scripture from James—the breakdown of the dangers of the tongue—and mediate on how it can destroy or build up so easily.

After you do this, talk about it. See, everyone who has a tongue has these issues. Pray, then take some time to write a sentence of your own together, a statement that you can agree upon that will unify your hopes at times when one or both of you begin to get heated.

We all stumble in many ways. Anyone who is never at fault in what they say is perfect, able to keep their whole body in check. When we put bits into the mouths of horses to make them obey us, we can turn the whole animal. Or take ships as an example. Although they are so large and are driven by strong winds, they are steered by a very small rudder wherever the pilot wants to go. Likewise, the tongue is a small part of the body, but it makes great boasts. Consider what a great forest is set on fire by a small spark. The tongue also is a fire, a world of evil among the parts of the body. It corrupts the whole body, sets the whole course of one's life on fire, and is itself set on fire by hell. All kinds of animals, birds, reptiles and sea creatures are being tamed and have been tamed by mankind, but no human being can tame the tongue. It is a restless evil, full of deadly poison. With the tongue we praise our Lord and Father, and with it we curse human beings, who have been made in God's likeness. Out of the same mouth come praise and cursing. My brothers and sisters, this should not be. Can both fresh water and salt water flow from the same spring? My brothers and sisters, can a fig tree bear olives, or a grapevine bear figs? Neither can a salt spring produce fresh water.

James 3:2–12

DAY 15: LOVE IS PATIENT

So many people say the reason they don't attend church, follow God, or haven't come to faith is because Christians are hypocrites. We have set a bad example, and whatever it is we have done, these people hold onto their prejudices and use them as a badge of evidence to justify their distance from Christ. Because we are seeking to get to the truth in this book, let's be honest and direct and say that it is actually only Christians who can be the "true hypocrites." We are the ones who know the truth, should be perfect, and have everything figured out because of what we find in our "little book" and how often we attend church and go on about our Savior.

These people have little room for grace and are not watching to see us grow more and more into Christ's image, literally "being perfected." Instead, they would rather we fail than make any sort of progress. Because this is the chapter after anger, and you have had two days to discuss why you may get angry and what may be the expression of it, it makes sense that we begin today with the topic of patience.

Paul launches into his famous love verse, describing what would seem to be some amazing expressions of faith.

> If I give away all I have, and if I deliver up my body to be burned, but have not love, I gain nothing.
>
> *1 Corinthians 13:3, ESV*

Willing to give all earthly possessions away, even heading to the grave, this is not enough to accomplish what God has for us in this life. Even after all that, which would surely bear witness and testify to many, if we have not love, we gain nothing.

Amazingly and directly, he begins verse 4 with "love is patient." See, if God has already said don't sin when we're angry, what should jump out to us is our

69

need to be patient. When I am angry, having the worst day, ready to let someone have it, without love expressed through patience, I will lose it. In all those angry situations in the past, if my wife and I had stopped, considered, and breathed for a moment, seeking to be patient, we would have been more considerate, would have had more understanding, and could have worked things out.

It's in this area that the world looks at us and throws our witness away because they have no room for patience with us. It's here that in the midst of intense situations at work, school, playing sports, or with my spouse, that emotion and expression take the lead over patience, even walking in love.

If we look at the story of Cain and Abel, what we see is a relationship lacking patience, and one that changes both men's lives for eternity.

Then the Lord said to Cain, "Where is your brother Abel?" "I don't know," he replied. "Am I my brother's keeper?" (Genesis 4:9). Imagine if when Cain, before he had murdered his brother Abel, would have asked himself if he was his brother's keeper. Of course he was his keeper; they were made for fellowship and friendship. But when Cain's sacrifice is rejected, "The LORD said to Cain, 'Why are you angry? Why is your face downcast? If you do what is right, will you not be accepted? But if you do not do what is right, sin is crouching at your door; it desires to have you, but you must rule over it'" (Genesis 4:6–7). He could have practiced patience—patience when his sacrifice was rejected, patience when his face was downcast, patience when sin was crouching at his door. There would have been no murder, no bloodshed; instead, we would have seen love play out its role in patience.

For this story to be significant at the beginning of the Bible, yet still be spoken of four thousand years later and ring true today, I guess we should have learned our lesson by now.

Paul said, "If I ... have not love, I gain nothing" (1 Corinthians 13:3, ESV). He doesn't gain, go on to maturity, learn how to overcome, profit from his mistakes, or experience transformation into the image of Christ.

Yes, Christ saved us, but He is still at work in us as He sanctifies us until the day we die.

If only our neighbors, those looking in on us, those considering our lives, were patient with us as we struggle forward, while they play loud music at all hours, their kids put a baseball through our windshield, or their dog thinks our lawn is his for leaving "little brown gifts" (not the kind purchased at See's Candies, I may add), wouldn't that be refreshing as we grow in our walk?

Yet, we often show this kind of patience to those looking in, the crazy neighbors, but can't learn to exercise this godly, loving patience with our spouses. More often than not, we treat our brother, sister, spouse as if Christ's work is finished, as if everything they do from here on out should be perfect, without any trace of failure.

Hmm ... "Love is patient," or we "gain nothing."

We see so many times how patience was the path that should have been walked in the lives of those in Scripture; but instead, it wasn't. Had Abraham and Sarah been patient with God's promise to bless them with a child, would Abraham have slept with his concubine Hagar, who gave birth to Ishmael? We still see the consequences of his actions today. Had Joseph not had patience, waiting upon the promises God had given him, to be raised up and rule and reign over his family and the nation, would he have sat patiently for thirteen years, trusting the Lord's plan to come to pass, and as a type of Christ, unite the twelve brothers, thereby protecting the nation from famine?

As I think back to first getting to know my wife, though we only dated for four months before we were married and though we spent every living second we could with one another, we had to be patient. What we see when getting to know our future spouse is two people who are complete opposites, despite what they may have in common, overlooking one another's faults and issues for the sake of what they believe will be a great bond and commitment. We had many conversations and faced many challenges that we were patient about because we believed that they would work out and that our love would keep uniting us in agreement.

Not being believers and having being married for a year, with the arrival of our firstborn, one of the main strains that caused our home to fall apart was a lack of patience. We didn't have grace, we were not thinking for the best, and so we gave patience no place in our lives together. We were both hurting, and where earlier we would have listened to one another, would have believed for the best, and trusted patiently that we would go on to make the right choices, putting to death any bad habits, instead, we destroyed our growing bond.

Think of this: wouldn't your marriage be different if you gave your spouse the same amount of patience you did your boss, your coach, or those in your life that may seem to take precedence? At this time, you may well look over at your spouse, as if to agree that you need more patience, but even now considering your lack of patience, you instead defend yourself rather than being patient with this word. Let's ponder this for a moment and hold the mirror of accountability up to ourselves.

If we consider our battles, issues, and lack of patience, what is the Holy Spirit speaking to us through James?

> My brethren, count it all joy when you fall into various trials, knowing that the testing of your faith produces patience. But let patience have its perfect work, that you may be perfect and complete, lacking nothing.
>
> *James 1:2–4, NKJV*

Follow the sequence: the testing of your faith produces patience and uses patience to finish its work. He's telling us that as things challenge us, as we allow patience to work in the midst of apparent chaos, it is for our good, on purpose, that we "may be perfect and complete, lacking nothing."

As Christ is at work in our lives, shaping and forming us, teaching us to be less like ourselves and more like Him, one of the ways He does this is by giving us things to be patient about. Imagine if we approached our issues with the mindset that God is using them for our good, like He promises in Romans 8:28–29. Practically, this means the longer you have lived, the longer you have been married, and the more challenges you have faced, if you have allowed patience to have its work, you will be more "perfect and complete, lacking nothing."

This past week I heard of two couples, families I have known for some time, who have been around church, ministry, and Christianity, looking every bit as believers (and I honestly mean that). Yet right now, as things have challenged their idea of marriage, as they have been let down, even without infidelity, they are on their way to separating.

Here's a good place for people to say, *Who are we to judge? Why is the church so serious about such issues?* Can I just liberate you? Let's just forget about the church for a moment; this is the Word of God. He is saying this for our good, and the church as a body should give godly advice and counsel so that couples can remain together and God can use patience for both His and the couple's good.

I live in a three-bedroom house of 1,700 square feet in California. My wife homeschools our three kids, and I generally do the majority of studying and prepping from home. Our days are up and down, depending on our schedule. But I can promise you this: when you live in a house with yourself, your wife, a thirteen-year-old, six-year-old, and a three-year-old, you will have many opportunities every day to exercise patience ... or not. I see it on my children's faces, my wife's face, and more often than not, on my own. Welcome to Christianity, the walk we are given, and the very situation God births us into, for His purpose.

In closing today, let's loosen up the mood, let's relax with one another, and let's confess to one another some of the ways we ourselves get mad, get frustrated, and miss our opportunity to let patience do its work in our lives, relationships, and witness. Just as we came up with a line to help us with our anger, the next step after assessing our situations and mood is to step into patience and trust the Lord.

DAY 16: LOVE IS KIND

So we've gotten into a blowout, a meltdown, argument, fight, and we've gone over in our mind or even verbally that we know better and need to exercise patience, and we allow it to take its course. As the mood in the room changes and the blood begins to cool down, *those thoughts* begin to linger: "She always starts it;" "He always goes too far;" "If this happens *one more time.*"

We get bombarded, our mind tries to place what just happened, and it's here that we can allow what just took place to have an effect on our character. They say our thoughts create channels and patterns that become familiar and that what we allow to fill our heads will soon direct our paths.

What paths are you allowing to be shaped? What paths are you directing over the ones the Holy Spirit inside of you is eager to shape?

Right after "love is patient," we are told that "love is kind." I don't know about you, but generally after people have been attacked or gotten into it, normally you don't see too many expressions of kindness following. Can I get an "Amen"?

As we grow into a more mature follower of Christ, we should be more familiar with how the Holy Spirit is eager for us to bear the "fruit" of His dwelling inside of us, and how this deferring to His ways will begin to establish new patterns.

It was mid-2013, and I was preaching at our home church through the Minor Prophets. Most people don't even know where to find Nahum and Obadiah, but I had been asked to speak on both of them in one service. Yikes! As I was praying before studying, I really felt God was leading me toward preaching on bitterness and how these books both showed wrongdoing being brought against a people whose response would have been in retaliation to their current situations. Over and over God reminds His people how He is the one who will handle the situations, how He is the one who will one day pour out His wrath.

My wife was out, and I had taken a break in between studying to do the dishes; my youngest son Jude (three) and my daughter Eden (six) were playing in the living room. Somewhere in the chaos of siblings interacting, I heard a loud "SMACK," as my son's heavy hand landed across his sister's face. Considering their ages and my hands being stuck in a sink full of dishes, I looked around to see what happened.

He caught her good, and she was ready to go. "Dad, Jude hit me! What are you going to do?" As she asked, and as I look down at my hands covered in dish soap, this whole picture of taking matters into our own hands, retaliating and being bitter flashed before my very eyes.

Before I had time to do anything as far as parenting my children, Eden lets out a "fine," and struts over to her brother, unleashing some of her own wrath. "SMACK," she connects with a mighty swing as he falls backward hitting the couch and then the floor.

Oh, parenting! Is it our kids who are meant to be learning something or us? For me that day I did learn something, or rather it just became more evident.

Had my daughter allowed for dad to compose himself, enter the situation, and give direction, we would have ended up with one child having been attacked; but instead, by taking matters into her own hands and unleashing the Old Testament style of an eye for an eye and a tooth for a tooth (Exodus 21:24), we ended up with two children facing the oncoming wrath. Not only had they hurt one another, but they also were about to be spending some quality time in separate parts of the house in timeouts.

Mom came home to clean dishes, a tidy house, everything in order, but with two children not getting to quite enjoy the day as they should have. And that's exactly what we get when we respond or react to our spouse with a lack of kindness.

Just as love is a choice, so it is to be patient and kind.

I wonder how our marriages would look if, regardless of our spouse's walks or behaviors, we lived on purpose to be kind. The definition of kindness is this: *to show yourself mild, being kind, using kindness.*

I know personally for me, kindness has been one of the biggest ways I have been able to show my wife I am committed and making the effort in our marriage. Yes, we said "I do," yes, we wear rings. We even have three children, a cat and a dog, but in the mix of daily happenings, as all is moving forward, it is kindness that really speaks to her of my efforts to lead and shape our home.

Being kind when it's that time of the month, being kind when homeschool has overwhelmed everyone that day, being kind when all the bills have landed, when I am tired, and when no one in the house wants to get into the flow of what God has set before us.

See, years ago, when we fought like crazy, kindness was spent, and there wasn't an eagerness for faith and grace to be in our conversation. But today, every word spoken, deed acted upon, and motive by which we are moved in kindness is speaking life for us.

We see kindness throughout the pages of Scripture in word and deed: kindness by serving, kindness by saying, kindness by doing. Just as we can say love is a feeling, as in something that cannot be defined but felt, love can be expressed, and it's in being kind that we can express it.

We can say that God is kind to us, in that while we were yet sinners, Christ died for us. God is kind to us, in that after we fell in the garden, He had in mind a plan to redeem us. God is kind to us because His love is felt through His continued acts of kindness toward us.

Because your kindness to one another is based solely on your interactions with one another, as you consider the verses below, ask in what ways you can better demonstrate your love in kindness.

Those who are kind benefit themselves, but the cruel bring ruin on themselves.

Proverbs 11:17

Therefore, as we have opportunity, let us do good to all people, especially to those who belong to the family of believers.

Galatians 6:10

DAY 17: ENVY, BOASTING, AND PRIDE

How dangerous, when we consider the world we live in, and how often we resemble it so well. As I read the Word of God, getting to this passage here in 1 Corinthians 13:4 that love "does not envy, does not boast, it is not proud," who else can this text point to any more than Satan himself?

Created by God, believed to be the lead worship angel close in proximity to the presence of God, what was it that took him (Satan) out of that position and forever distanced their relationship to one that will end in flames, literally?

His own passions, desires, and needs were the fuel that gave room for him to pursue the various paths of sin.

As we take these words to heart—envy, boasting, and pride—one of the consistent patterns is that they are all tied into having or not having, being satisfied or not satisfied with exactly what is intended. Yes, "intended." God created us and birthed us into this world exactly on time, and He is currently at work in our marriages that they might represent Him as best they can. I know I already stated this, but let me ask you: Who is the greatest hindrance to this witness? Is it Satan, through whom we trace fallen man back to, or is it ourselves who, even after hearing of God's plan, still chose to eat of the fruit (represented by what Adam and Eve did in the garden of Eden)?

You see, since starting this book, three of the couples I have been connecting with were headed for divorce, even to the extent of signing papers. They met, fell in love, came into their marriage with all kinds of motivated and positive plans of love, romance, sex, a future, a home, kids, and a happily ever after. They had in mind something they built, fashioned, and planned. Yet now, as things fall apart, as money is spent on things like diapers, time is spent resting because of long hours working to provide or catching up on the late nights of nursing, suddenly the end picture doesn't look as good as it first did. Whose fault is that? Did we come into marriage to be led by God, or did we paint a picture so big that anything other than this picture looks like we are settling for less?

How can I possibly tie in how Satan was separated from God to how we ourselves can walk in his very footsteps in our own marriages? Well, consider that God had a very specific plan in mind for Lucifer, later named Satan, and that plan was to play music that places God at the center. Lucifer took his eyes off both God and God's plan and decided upon his own ways; he no longer wanted to worship someone else (God); instead, he wanted others to bow down and worship him.

> "How you are fallen from heaven, O Day Star, son of Dawn! How you are cut down to the ground, you who laid the nations low! You said in your heart, 'I will ascend to heaven; above the stars of God I will set my throne on high; I will sit on the mount of assembly in the far reaches of the north; I will ascend above the heights of the clouds; I will make myself like the Most High.' But you are brought down to Sheol, to the far reaches of the pit."
>
> *Isaiah 14:12–15,* ESV

In this well-known verse, known as the five "I wills," we see that Lucifer, this "fallen" one, originally began his walk on the right foot, partaking in what God had planned for him. Amazing. But soon, because of what was in his heart, he was "brought down to Sheol, to the far reaches of the pit …"

To level with you today, opening up about my marriage, I can count on two hands, just since beginning this book, how many times my marriage may well have felt like it was being brought "down to Sheol," even to "the far reaches of the pit;" and why? Because of envy, boasting, and pride. And this will forever be a daily battle my wife and I will face.

Living as a professional skateboarder, with bills being paid by sponsors from products and for events, began to slow down these past few years as my focus turned from a life of tricks and travel to one of the Gospel call. This has definitely affected our lives.

Now in my mid-thirties, I am pastoring at a church called Rock Harbor in Huntington Beach, California, while still being freed up to travel for ministry that comes up in schools, recovery programs, outreaches, and church events. But at the same time I have a stay-at-home-wife who homeschools our three children, we live in California, and we need to pay our bills.

Do you see where I am going? A smaller salary, in part from church, in part from love offerings, and in part from people who choose to support this ambiguous position of somewhat urban missionary, as they feel led.

And this life of skateboarding, though we didn't live extravagantly or desire things that would be perishing, we did have our comforts. And now as I lose that comfort of knowing exactly what enters the bank each month, or as my wife may not be able to plan to do this or that, therein enters "envy, boasting, and pride."

As a man concerned about the finances, I find myself beginning to undermine the things my wife does with our money rather than the things I do. "Why is she focused on this and that? Shouldn't she do things my way, since I know better?"

Seeing other people and the stages of life they are in, it suddenly jumps out how together some people have it and how, when listening to the flesh, my future doesn't feel secure. They live here, have this and that, and their kids are set.

As these thoughts meander around my head, I begin to envy; I boast, and in my pride, I begin to speak and argue about how things should be for us, all the while missing what God may well be trying to do in us.

For Tracy, she is fed the same old lies, as the magazines hit the doorsteps, the television rolls on, and the Internet flexes its idolatrous muscles. Will you have the kitchen you want and deserve? They will! Will your kids' outfits look Pinterest-picture-perfect worthy every day, and maybe get enough likes to land on the trending Instagram page—the one with all the celebrities on it? Will you hit your 60s looking like you're in your 40s while having lived the most fulfilled life every second of every day? See, as ridiculous as some of these things sound, since Satan fell, all he has been trying to do is distract us from the main goal and have us follow his path of self-seeking and self-glorification over God's.

These past six months have brought up more than enough arguments between me and Tracy as we have prayed and looked forward to our family's future and possible next season.

So we don't have it down pat. Things get especially hard when the envy of the comfort we once felt just a few years back sneaks in, or when the boasting of how we should have done things speaks loudly as we remind the other of their lack of understanding, and especially when the pride of having to have it my own way is first and foremost where I speak from.

See, for the Christian, we don't walk around being prideful, boastful, and envious of the things we once did before Christ. Instead, we hold on to this idea and can manipulate circumstances through Lucifer's tactics while not submitting to the Lord.

But as I think of this season, and the things my wife and I tried to work through, it was when we most resembled Satan's ways most that our evenings ended up feeling more like a pit than an oasis.

What am I saying? That your circumstances will change and the conditions too, but how you respond to them and learn to handle them does not need to be unloving. Paul goes on in his letter to the church in Corinth saying that love "does not dishonor others, it is not self-seeking, it is not easily angered, it keeps no record of wrongs" (1 Corinthians 13:5)

For me and my wife, it was through circumstances changing that caused us to have to make changes. When we dishonored one another, were self-seeking, were angered, and turned to our record of wrongs stored in our heads, we missed our moments of love. But isn't that, after all, what life is all about?

I know we have looked at some of these topics earlier, but for tonight, I suggest that individually, we take some alone time to sit in private prayer and ask God to show us what things in our hearts we envy, are selfish about, that we boast of, and even take pride in. Maybe even take a notepad or journal to write down things that come to mind that you may already know of or that the Holy Spirit presents.

Prepare to get alone with God for at least fifteen minutes.

Come to Him as His child, knowing He has already paid the full price and cannot love us any more than what He has already showed us on the cross, as He gave His Son in our place.

Begin to thank Him for washing away your sins, for making a way for you to be forgiven, and for wanting you to reach out to Him as His sons and daughters. You, though you lost your way, have now been born again into His family.

This idea and mindset should bring you to a place of being able to openly come before Him to ask:

1. God, what is that I am envying that should have no part in my relationship with my spouse?

It could be a lifestyle, mindset, achievement, person, a position, or a grass-is-greener point of view.

2. What is it that I boast in that I didn't bring into this world, nor will I leave with it, be it an experience or a gift that I allow to steer me from humility?

3. What do I carry in my heart that allows me to be prideful, that doesn't represent You and may even hinder my marriage or witness?

Though these things seem ambiguous for yourself personally, you will know the things that you hold onto, will fight over, will get the blood flowing, and that will lead your discussions to get out of control and cause love to flee.

After this exercise, pray together as a couple and then let each one share what they felt was on their heart and that would be good to bring out into the open.

Don't accuse one another or remind one another, nodding the head or rolling the eyes as may seem fitting.

Simply bond and let God's Spirit do the work.

DAY 18: DOES NOT DELIGHT IN EVIL

We have been on our way now for well over two weeks. As I have been writing this, I have been getting all sorts of feedback from people who have felt the first seventeen chapters have opened them up to more and more discussions. They have seen how God's Word pertains to their marriages, but most importantly, how it pertains to their personal walks with the Lord.

We wrapped up yesterday by going through an exercise, asking God to show us some of the things that rise up in us and cause us to represent Satan more than Jesus. As we continue on into 1 Corinthians 13, we have to be aware of a few things: we are waging war, and the things we wrestle with are not just carnal and blatantly sinful, but they are also spiritual (Ephesians 6:10–18). We have to break the cycle and patterns that try to reform in our minds. Jesus has already delivered us, but we can fall into old mindsets.

Paul gives us a good reminder as he begins to conclude his verse on love. He's just pointed out what's wrong: that we envy, boast, and are prideful. Here he begins by summing it all up: "Love does not delight in evil" (1 Corinthians 13:6).

Now, who in their right mind would want to delight in evil? But I can remember those years of despair when my marriage was failing, even when we were apart, and even at times while getting back together trying to make it work, when that cycle of having to get the last word or show my wife where she was wrong became so necessary when things got out of hand. Literally, my desire to be right, or be the one in control, would cause me to fall into this pattern that God calls "evil."

As I've said before, it's great for me to be everywhere sharing my testimony about how God restored our marriage, but that has nothing to do with the fact that He is still restoring it every day and that this work is continuous.

Because it's a continuous process, I have to daily decide never to delight in evil, which as we will see, is not just spooky films, upside-down crosses, and people shouting 666 while spewing blood from their mouth at a rock show. Yes, we have come to think of evil as something so ridiculous, when in actuality we see in verse 7 that the opposite of evil is love: "always protects, always trusts, always hopes, always perseveres."

James 4:17 says, he who "knows the good they ought to do and doesn't do it, it is sin." We take from this that at the times of conflict, there is a blatant pattern to follow so I do the opposite of that which is evil.

As an example, let's say I wasn't the one writing this book but the one reading it. Could I possibly by now, through reading these chapters, have had some things exposed, brought to light, or made known that have caused me to doubt, give up, or look for a way out of my marriage? If Tracy and I are going through a hard time where it is difficult to forgive or I am reminded daily of how much greener the grass may seem in some other situation, how do I flee from evil? How can I ensure that my marriage will be airtight and actually walk in the faith I claim to have?

See, it's one thing to have faith when things are good, but another thing when situations are worse than ever and there seems to be no light in sight. It is here that we will let all hell break loose, literally; and as Paul says, we will be delighting in evil by not protecting, trusting, hoping, and persevering.

Before we were born again, right after the envy, boasting, and pride had taken root in our arguments, next came the verbal wars, the past brought up, the projected future failures, and the lack of all hope ...

I don't personally believe that it is what we do in marriage per se that causes people to give up and compromise their faith, but that it is the methods that we can use in relating to one another that allows things to get out of control to the extent that we don't see love as a safeguard to help our fights subside. As I feel my blood boiling over and our tones begin to get louder or our words get shorter or more personal, it's here that we have to "depart from evil," that we have to trust God not to "lead us not into temptation." And we need to remind ourselves that love does always protect, trust, hope, and persevere.

I remember one of the first fights we got into after coming to faith and our remarriage. Having raised our voices enough to know we needed to cool down, as I was walking out of our living room into the bedroom, these words came to mind, "Are you protecting, trusting, hoping?" followed by the suggestion to go back into the room and hug and kiss her. Really? Why would I do that?

I'm mad; she's mad; we don't want to hug and kiss right now. We don't want to be close; it doesn't feel "romantic" or worthwhile to do such things, especially when nothing in our faces or body language shows it.

But this is exactly when I need to learn to walk in God's promises—when my flesh has had enough and my body wants no part of my spouse that moment. It's right here that we get to see the Holy Spirit at work, not because we feel like it but because these are the extraordinary moments that aren't seen in the movies or on TV. It is within these normal moments that we see God at work the most in our marriages.

As I turned around, exiting the bedroom, approaching my wife, putting an arm around her, kissing her on the forehead, she knew it was uncomfortable for me, even out of place so suddenly. But who did it bring glory to first and make the center of our chaos at that second? God!

I look back on that day as a reminder. When times of strife or angst arise, I now see open doors for spouses to express *protection*, *trust* in what the future will look like, *hope* in the God who leads, and *perseverance* through the thick and the thin that we committed to through our marriage vows before God and many other witnesses.

Yes, it is uncomfortable. But that's why the Holy Spirit is referred to as the Comforter. It's His responsibility, not ours, to show up and move in our spouse's heart. Our responsibility is in the obedience of changing our attitude that, by default is evil, and instead doing things God's way.

Oh, I get that we are "born again," that we have confessed, read our Bibles, and have the Christian walk almost down pat. But I'm talking about here, right in the midst of your daily meltdowns and carnal moments, actually trusting this very verse to protect, trust, hope, and persevere.

It's only when we truly recklessly abandon the world's mindset and mold, and rather choose to do things God's way and put on the mind of Christ that we can be aligned with the Scriptures and say "Love never fails."

There's no clearer way to look at it tonight. The way the world handles disputes is not by choosing to protect, trust, hope, and persevere, as things get heated.

But we are not like the world. Jesus called us out of the world. Romans 12:2 tells us, "Do not conform to the pattern of this world." Be nothing like it; shake off these moments of fleeing, of walking in evil rather than in faith, and walk out your struggles God's way.

This is a process, something we apply ourselves to. And at its core is a sign of spiritual maturity as we are being transformed "by the renewing" of our minds (Romans 12:2).

It's sad to me that we can give so much time to the training and discipline it takes to get the job we want or to know every detail about our favorite football teams. Even after we first meet our spouses, our time is constantly consumed with thoughts of them and their best interests.

But imagine if today, we were more consumed with God and what we read about Him. More consumed with Jesus and the mind He has given us to walk in. More consumed with the Holy Spirit and the power we have been given as He daily abides in us, His children.

It's then (and only then), as we flex our spiritual muscles in Christ, that our spouse will see the benefits of God's promises as the biblical presentation of "Love never fails."

Between you and your spouse, talk through and pray about some ways that you personally feel you have shut down, pulled back, or given in when you should have instead turned to the Holy Spirit and trusted Him to lead you to protect, trust, hope, and persevere.

Read over the verse below, even praying over one another, aware that as you begin to change the way you resolve your conflicts, you are literally able to "test and approve what God's will is."

Do not conform to the pattern of this world, but be transformed by the renewing of your mind. Then you will be able to test and approve what God's will is—his good, pleasing and perfect will.

Romans 12:2

DAY 19: TRUST WHO?

When I think of my life, my walk, and my marriage, I would have to say that one of the things that has been hard for me to do is trust.

We live in a world where people expect to be trusted, as if trusting them is their right. But since I can remember, as is probably the same for you, my stories, even from childhood, involve people lying, deceiving, and bending the truth, if even for so-called justified reasons. But honestly, is there really such a thing as a white lie; aren't they all lies? Is there a way to not answer truthfully, or are we still being deceptive? Is there a way to get what you want without manipulating? The answer is obvious!

Even while reading this, I imagine there are already personal situations or experiences coming to your mind. If you are like me, you've seen people ripped off, cheated, deceived in a business deal, or straight up targeted, so why would you trust anyone?

For me, I wasn't so much afraid to open up to people or allow them into my life for a lack of trust; it's that I expected people to be sideways, to sooner or later overstep their boundaries, function in their own best interests and do me wrong, even though I was believing for the best.

The reason this didn't matter so much to me was because these people would be in and out of my life. It wasn't as if I was living with them, interacting with them daily, or committing to a lifelong journey, like I would in marriage.

When I met Tracy, I was aware that she was coming out of a prior relationship. I was in America focusing mostly on my skate career and not a Christian. And I had already engaged with other people prior to meeting her. We had been dating for four months and were about to be married, but was I ready to trust, commit, and believe this person for life and agree to be trustworthy myself?

When you think about all that goes into marriage, how little we really think about what we are promising. Every experience we have had is bending us toward who we are as we make this commitment.

Think about it; literally every interaction with every female in my life, from girls I thought were cute and had crushes on in school, to dating, being in relationships with, all from my early teens to now almost into my twenties. All those I had flirted with, thought of as pretty, and more. Every image that had been put before my eyes, even of the pornographic kind as my friends passed around their dad's magazines as teens or were purchased at the many gas stations as we journeyed across America and the world skateboarding. All of these experiences had created in me a foundation that was not of or for God. Also, and even more to the point, as I was beginning to date my wife, there were plenty of guys who were flirting with her at the Mother's Market restaurant where she worked daily.

Would these habits of ours continue on into our marriage? How do we draw borders, or as they are known biblically, put up "hedges of protection"?

To align these lifelong experiences alongside the Bible, which tells us that no one is good except God alone (Romans 3:12), that all have sinned (Romans 3:23), and that every inclination of the thoughts of the human heart was only evil all the time (Genesis 6:5), it's very easy to understand why people have such a hard time trusting anyone.

Yet, right here in Paul's famous verse, we are told "love ... always trusts," and in our marriages, we are called to love. Am I saying to trust while your spouse is out cheating, flirting with every co-worker, or living for his or herself? No, I am not saying to trust in them, but I am saying to trust in God, in the work He may well do in them.

See, the focus is less on the person, your spouse, but more on the belief of what God has called you to do in your walk, as you shine the light of Christ by loving them. Your trust, then, is more about walking out your walk with God, and if you didn't already know this, this is exactly what your walk is anyway.

The day you confessed Jesus as Lord, the Holy Spirit moved on your heart and showed you your sin nature, bringing you to repentance. Those very words you cried out, "Forgive me, Lord," "thank You Jesus," and so forth were not just random sentences, but words of faith, hope, belief, and trust. Romans 10:9–10 says, "if you confess with your mouth that Jesus is Lord and believe in your heart that God raised him from the dead, you will be saved" (ESV). Well, confessing and believing is trusting, so your walk, your prayer, your Christianity began with trust, and so it continues.

We see in Scripture that Abraham, the "father of faith," has this title because he believed God, trusted Him, and hoped in Him. How can a man one hundred years of age possibly have a child without trust? Let alone that his wife, Sarah, was ninety and probably had been through menopause twice over. Abraham believed God for a child, and God blessed him with a son named Isaac. This child of promise, through whom God would continue to bless the world, whose descendants became as numerous as the stars that light our night sky and the grains of sand that make up our beaches, would be in the very lineage by which the Messiah would come.

The Bible could have finished Abraham's story here, but it didn't. Abraham was given this child; then God challenged him to take Isaac up to the mountaintop as a sacrifice to the Lord.

As Abraham went in faith, finding the mountaintop location, building an altar, binding his son with rope, and even cocking his hand back, armed with a knife for the final devastating blow, the angel of the Lord interrupted Abraham:

> "Do not lay a hand on the boy … Now I know that you fear God, because you have not withheld from me your son, your only son."
>
> *Genesis 22:12*

Here is Abraham, thinking he would not have another child, but aware that God could raise Isaac from the dead (see Hebrews 11:19), aware that God could give him another son, putting off his emotions and motives, with fear and reverence for God, choosing to TRUST Him. Abraham, by the way, came out of a pagan heritage. So to not have a son to continue your lineage was disgraceful. What would his life amount to? Who would he leave behind after he was gone?

Not only did God bless Abraham, He also provided a ram caught in the thicket by its horns, symbolic of how God's own Son, Jesus Christ, would one day be caught/nailed to a cross/thicket, as the once-and-for-all sacrifice for all mankind. Right here in Genesis we are given this beautiful picture of how we are to trust God and believe Him by His Word, while walking in faith through whatever the daily circumstances will look like.

This is how it is for us in marriage. Since being first married and aware of people who would flirt with my wife or seeing how doors could open that could harm our marriage, did I have any control over the outcome? Since traveling the world touring before I was a believer and seeing how easy it is for trust to be broken and for situations to become sinful, now, as believers, we both have had to understand that we cannot control nor predict the future.

In the same way that Abraham trusted God with Isaac, I also have to trust God with my spouse. Noah trusted God that it would rain after he had been building the ark for one hundred years. Moses trusted God to lead Israel out of Egyptian bondage or to part the Red Sea. David trusted God as he slayed a lion, bear, and even Goliath. Daniel trusted as he was thrown into the lion's den. And we can go on and on all the way up to Jesus, who trusted God with every prayer, every word of faith, and even as He sweated blood at Gethsemane, petitioning God, "My Father, if it is possible, may this cup be taken from me. Yet not as I will, but as you will" (Matthew 26:39).

Everything that Jesus did was by faith, believing and trusting God. And if we don't walk in our marriages this way, we won't have any foundation to ensure the stability needed.

Jesus knew Judas would betray Him but He continued to do exactly what He was called to do, loving him and bearing witness to him.

As you and your spouse move forward in your marriage, even though there may be doubts about things confessed in times past, habits that have not been worked out, or issues that are constantly arising, making it so very difficult to trust, my suggestion to you today is let go of your spouse. Begin to trust God for them. Don't be distant from them, but literally, pray them before God's throne tonight, and trust God to work in them.

We need to believe and trust today that as you both agree to work toward a more godly marriage, having Christ at the center, you can both agree on His ways and paths in your hearts.

A good friend of mine, whose wife recently filed for divorce, has had the absolute hardest time working toward reconciliation. How can he trust her? How can anything she says actually be taken seriously? And within a few months of their time apart, she came around wanting the marriage to work, getting counsel, and realizing divorce was not God's plan. She still has not cancelled the divorce but is well aware that it does not go forward until they sign off on it. But for him, this has become a giant weight that hangs over him and stops him from focusing on being the very man in this marriage God has called him to be.

I fully understand this. I have been in those situations in my marriage when all the wind has been taken from me, when I have woken up in the middle of the night anxious, sweating, struggling with something we were facing, but what can we do? How do we handle this? By trusting, believing, bearing what may be, hoping for the best, and enduring.

I have no doubt that by the time this book is finished, their divorce will be called off, and they will be well on their way to a more godly future. But for now, they are both trusting and believing that the struggles and challenges they are still facing are being worked out in the Lord.

Disclaimer: If your spouse is off running about, doing all kinds of crazy things, spending more time focused on themselves than God, you, or your family, I am not writing this to empower them to continue with the way they are living.

In fact, if this is you reading this, and you are off on your own agenda, you need to repent tonight and realize that God will judge all people. On one hand, He is a loving Father to those who hear His voice and follow Him, but to those who don't, His wrath will one day be poured out; and I can assure you, all the pleasures and self-satisfaction you are gaining temporarily now, what is to come for all eternity will far outweigh them in the most terrible way possible.

This is not a scare tactic, but it is the scary truth.

God's grace and mercy are for you today, and I pray He grabs your heart, convicts you, and leads you to repentance. You were made for so much more, and this marriage is where He is most going to work in you and unto others.

Tonight, I recommend taking some time to share with one another, even writing down some of the things that have made you insecure and unable to trust one another in times past, some of the things that have hurt you or that you have held on to that need to be addressed.

This will help your spouse, who is meant to be there for support and to love and protect you, to see some of the areas that they can go out of their way to help make you feel more loved, be it by their not doing something, or helping you to understand what really happened or the intention.

It is very important to be able to listen and ask yourself if you are really there for one another.

Also, what's important is to choose tonight to commit one another to God, to trust Him first because He will "never leave you nor forsake you" (Joshua 1:5). It's Him who needs to be the center and rock in your marriage, not your spouse.

Then, pray together for your commitments to one another.

Begin to speak God's promises over your marriage, your covenant, your future.

Thank God for the work He is doing and will continue to do. Believe for the best, regardless of your current situation.

DAY 20: THE BOOK OF LOVE[1]

So you are twenty chapters in. You have made it this far; what exactly is happening in your life, walk, marriage, and relationship to date? What do the results look like? Has anything changed?

You may well be sitting here saying "no," if the answer you are looking for is that life is easy and marriage is simply a stroll in the park. But remember, our purpose is not to fix your life; it is to help you and your spouse understand one another in light of God's plan.

Recently, while counseling a man who is in a struggling marriage, I asked him, "How much of you has died since you got married?" to which he stopped and paused. Was he still working for his own ways, or was he holding fast to God's?

My point was not to make him feel like he was walking around wounded, hurt, and on his way out, but instead to see how much of himself has been changed through understanding and dependence upon the Holy Spirit, as he has applied God's Word to this difficult season of his life.

Today, friends, before we head into the final ten chapters of this book, it would be wise to take inventory, do a checkup on where we are in the goal and purpose of picking up this book to begin with.

As I said from the start, this book is broken down into three main sections: the first ten chapters focusing on doctrine, understanding God's plan and purpose for our lives; the next ten chapters digging more into the practical ways we are together as one directed by God's Word, finishing off by opening up 1 Corinthians 13:4–8 on love never failing; and finally, the last ten chapters being on the more personal ways you and your spouse interact based on what current issues I have experienced or seen in marriages at this time.

---

[1] The Monotones. "The Book of Love." *Who Wrote the Book of Love?* Mascot, 1957.

Before turning this corner, we need to again hold fast to our mission statement, "love never fails." It cannot! Jesus did the most loving thing ever—dying for our sins. And though the odds were against Him, He never failed as He walked with trust in His Father and the Holy Spirit's anointing, thus fulfilling the Word.

So for you and your spouse today, supposing you are both eagerly believing for your marriage, or even if one is thinking of choosing another path, how's it looking?

Have you personally been grasping a hold of and choosing to submit your body to the direction of His Word? Jesus, while speaking of the teachers of the law and the Pharisees, told us not to do what they did, for they did not practice what they preached (see Matthew 23:3). Have we been putting into practice what we ourselves are preaching in agreement with what we have read?

Here am I, the guy writing this book, but is everything about my marriage in its perfect place, always flowing smoothly, as if my wife and I have already ascended into heaven? No! For these past twenty days, I too have been holding fast to the promises of God as a doer of the word, not only a hearer (see James 1:22).

With this in mind, it would be healthy for us to walk alongside Paul the apostle himself for a moment. Here he is on his jolly way persecuting Christians left, right, and center when suddenly he falls to the ground, blinded by the light, and has a radical encounter with Jesus who then commissions him to become an apostle to the gentiles.

This Paul—a Hebrew of Hebrews, from the tribe of Benjamin, a Roman citizen who has been set apart by God, who, we could surely say on paper, would seem to have a leg up on all of us—invites us into his very own thoughts, as through confession we hear the condition of his heart.

> I do not understand what I do. For what I want to do I do not do, but what I hate I do.
>
> *Romans 7:15*

He even goes on to say, "What a wretched man I am! Who will rescue me from this body that is subject to death?" (Romans 7:24).

Paul, this man set apart, speaks of how he doesn't understand what he does, how the things he wants to do he doesn't do. Does this sound familiar? Could you replace his name with yours? I can. Do we walk toward things but end up arriving at another destination?

This is what our lives will look and feel like at times. But this mindset needs to be one of constantly maturing further and further away from the same patterns we have been stuck in. Meaning, twenty chapters in, our view of marriage should have changed. Twenty chapters in and my understanding of God's plan should be shaping my life. Twenty chapters in, and we should have understood that even our effort and goals along the way might well, if anything, have revealed what's really inside of us. Ouch!

When Paul speaks of being a *wretched man*, he is actually pointing to an old and disgusting form of torture. Prisoners of that day, depending on their crimes, might have had a dead corpse tied to their body. Imagine them literally carrying around this rotting flesh, with open wounds, the stench of decay, and to make it a bit more gruesome, body fluids, excretions, or even things like eyeballs falling out. Yuck! Why so detailed? Because this is what Paul is saying my walk is like: daily, I wander around with the dead version of Brian, the old man I used to be attached to me.

Picture it for yourself. Imagine the new you dragging along the dead version of you. And these dead bodies, stinking and wreaking of death, still want the things of this world over the things of God.

It is no longer I who live but Christ (Galatians 2:20), speaking of the death of my flesh, while Christ leads me by the Holy Spirit.

"Old things have passed away; behold, all things have become new," we are told, speaking of what took place upon being born again (2 Corinthians 5:17, NKJV). Moving forward we are now to "put off your old self, which belongs to your former manner of life and is corrupt through deceitful desires, and to be renewed in the spirit of your minds, and to put on the new self, created after the likeness of God in true righteousness and holiness" (Ephesians 4:22–24, ESV).

Paul's point in Romans 7 is to show us that there are now two laws at work, two voices, if you like, and twenty chapters in, which voice have you been listening to? The old man and what may feel right, or the new man in Christ and who can prosper your marriage as you take this step in the upcoming chapters to the more personal sides of your covenant?

My point is to show you that regardless of where you both may be today, as long as you are moving forward, you are in good company.

Have these twenty chapters worn you out or shed light where there was too much darkness? Have one of you made all the effort while the other seems to be sitting on the fence?

What we need to do tonight is to take a breather, realize that God is still in control, and remind ourselves that it isn't twenty chapters of some book, or forty, for that matter, that is going to radically change our lives. It's God Himself. He is still the potter and the one at work in this life we live.

Tonight would be a good night to recoup, consider the expectations we may have put on our spouse, or even ourselves, and like Paul, we need to stop and remember just how much we need God's mercy and grace.

Paul is the one rhetorically asking after all, "What a wretched man I am! Who will rescue me from this body that is subject to death?" And he does not leave us hanging, but answers, "Thanks be to God, who delivers me through Jesus Christ our Lord!" (Romans 7:24–25).

Thanks be to God, thanks be to God, the Lord, wherever we are today, wherever those reading this book are in both location, in life, in marriage, and in thought.

Lord, You are still on the throne, and there is still time. And whatever fights may have come up, or where situations may have been brewing causing offense, God, You are still available to lead and direct. Lord, we give over our spouses to You tonight and trust that You know what is going on and that You are the one we can trust, have faith in, and depend upon.

God, tonight would You give us peace and the joy that surpasses all understanding, as we place both ourselves and our spouses in Paul's shoes, saying, *What a wretched man/woman, I am! Who will rescue me from this body that is subject to death?*

And God, we say thank You tonight. Thank You that only You can deliver us, and only You can continue the work in our hearts and the hearts of our spouses.

We know we can ask, trust, and rest at this time because You went to the cross for us. You went to the cross for our lives, and You went to the cross for the promises concerning our marriages. We let go of our expectations, accept what You are trying to accomplish, and we choose to continue to love because "love never fails."

DAY 21: NO, YOU CHANGE!

I don't care how hard you try, how much effort you give, or how much time you put in; you won't be able to do it. Change your mate, that is! People have had their whole lives to be conditioned the way they are. Plus, we are born with sin natures. Yet, we still make the effort, even hanging our satisfaction and the state of our marriages upon who we are hoping our spouses will become.

Now, if you have been married for any longer than two years, by now you understand that both you and your spouse are completely different people from when you were first married.

How did this change occur? Was it because you brought your agenda into the marriage and began to control your spouse? Or have the circumstances of your marriage, both good and bad, caused growth, made you consider, struggle, grow, consider, and grow some more?

This past week, a couple on the verge of a failing marriage, who have everything to gain by staying together, are both operating in survival mode. Because of stubbornness, bitterness, and being worn throughout these few years of chaos, they are not able to move forward unless they first see a change in their spouse.

Their problem: both have been raised with ideas of the perfect spouse. Their parents set the standard so high and now, anyone less than perfect becomes hard to love. The sigh or gasp that I daily hear come out of their mouths due to not having this ideal life is exactly what is stopping them from dying to self and giving their all. This, by the way, is actually what they want to be able to do. So the end result is they're being deceived, living to see their spouse changed rather than living to give them love.

And it's here that they will miss where God is actually at work.

Recently, I was in downtown Huntington Beach amidst the world famous U.S. Open surfing contest. It's sad that it isn't even the surfing or skating that the event is becoming known for. Instead, it is becoming known for how our youth, kids who are barely in their teens, are running all over town almost naked, with writing all over themselves asking for hugs, or much cruder and more suggestive things. The articles that came out about the event were heavily focused on how so many of the younger kids were being groped and taken advantage of, almost as if it was the norm.

Taking all of this in, having three children of my own, it began to stir in my mind, "Whom will my kids marry?" "What will their spouses be like?" Because for these kids downtown, though it all seemed like fun and games, their level of respect, dignity, and decency was being torn to pieces in such a way that any idea of a godly spouse was left wanting.

It makes me think, even as a Christian today, if I were not married to Tracy and were to marry someone else, would it be any easier after now living the life I have lived and experiencing the things I have, being more familiar with God's biblical perspective on marriage? While it's true in theory, that I am better equipped now, wouldn't I have to still walk it out? Are there not the exact same numbers of hours in the day or challenges in the week that are going to reveal the faults in both me and my imaginary spouse?

Everything these kids were experiencing downtown will be carried into their marriages. The people my kids will marry are, right now, somewhere in the world being formed and shaped. I can do all I can to prepare my kids to be biblical, have understanding, know the verses, strive to walk as Christ did, but when push comes to shove, two sinners in Christ are still going to have to live under one roof with the goal of riding out the storms of marriage and seeing Christ lifted up.

As we focus on loving our spouses for who they are rather than who we want them to be, I want to draw for you the two extremes. My own children could one day marry someone as biblically sound as is possible. But they could also marry one of these young people who were running around downtown, someone who will later come to Christ after having lived the hardest of lives. In both circumstances, both the command and solution is the same—love them.

Now don't get the idea that as I am writing these chapters, sounding like I am seated on the mountain of God with Moses, that I have all the answers. I am not any easier to love, for my spouse, than the next person.

When God puts people together, He is aware of what He is doing and is purposeful in using both the good and bad in that relationship to help both spouses to grow. If my goal is to change my spouse, it's only because I am unable to love them right where they are. "I love them," you say, but as discussed earlier, love is also an action. It does something, is alive, fluid, and moving. Can you love them where they are, in whatever state, knowing that the only change will come because of God's work in them? And that is the only change you should believe for anyway.

Of all the things I have experienced in this world, what I have learned is that I wish to be more Christlike every day. And in the midst of my life and what it throws at me, I want to be able to change so many things about myself. But if I were able to do this, in either my spouse or myself, where would the work of the Holy Spirit be? Where would the shaping by the Word or the comfort of God's unfailing love as I struggle in His work in me be?

As we look at the more practical side, I am asking you to give up trying to change your spouse, and to simply walk out your role as their spouse.

One thing I have learned through the years of skating is that you have to finish what you start. A deadline is set: for a video, to learn a trick, to shoot a photo, and you base all of your time, that day or week, on making sure it is accomplished. But within my marriage, after becoming a believer, I had to realize that loving my spouse was not simply making sure I stay married, as if it's some trick or task. But instead, I have to be present in the daily reality of loving her in the midst of the Holy Spirit's work. Loving her not with my focus being on the end, though that is set in stone in my mind, but loving the process, which, like in skating, includes the slams, shiners (ouch), and broken boards as I stay committed and focused on the outcome.

Today, take a step back and relax. Think through how, in the midst of this crazy world—where we are seeing a rise in terrorism, violent outbreaks across the U.S, all kinds of politically correct issues directing society, the fame and shame game, and the never-ending rat race—that you and your spouse are in the middle of your marriage and can already be a success by accepting one another just as you are, with all your issues, hidden or visible, as you simply love one another.

DAY 22: PRIORITY OR PRINCIPLE?

So you're still here, almost to the end of this book; we have established some truths and gained some ground. So now, practically and between the two of you, have you really made your marriage, after God, the priority of your lives?

See, we have heard the principles, we have seen the truths, but to actually get any substance from the text we have read off the pages and into our lives, it will take prioritizing. We are unfolding the principles, but the priority has to be the application—that's the driving force.

Consider the soccer player who learns everything about the game, but heads out onto the field of an actual match only to treat it as a practice. Or the worker who heads into his training, working hard enough to understand everything but underperforms once the store opens because the job is not actually their priority but simply a steppingstone to something else far off in the distance.

Don't we grow up looking at marriage as something so important (which it is); yet, after getting married, as time goes on, find that because we understand the principles, we think we are making it a priority? But that isn't the case (and correct me if I am wrong) if we don't give our all.

When Paul writes to the church in Corinth, he points out how great it is for those who are not married, as they can be fully focused on God all the more. He then lists how we should approach marriage in our walk with Christ.

> Marriage involves you in all the nuts and bolts of domestic life and in wanting to please your spouse, leading to so many more demands on your attention. The time and energy that married people spend on caring for and nurturing each other, the unmarried can spend in becoming whole and holy instruments of God.
>
> *1 Corinthians 7:33–34, THE MESSAGE*

Marriage involves "you," he says, in "all the nuts and bolts of domestic life." "In wanting to please your spouse, leading to so many more demands on your attention." Even saying, "the time and energy ... married people spend on caring for and nurturing each other," which implies this is a major part of their lives, as it should be.

My wife and I both need to apply this; it is not simply in the text. The reality is that my spouse is a living being, and she is in need of things that only I can give to her, even as there are things only she can give to me.

You might say, "Can't I live without my spouse?" Well, of course you can. But you are married, which means God has in mind (for all married couples) that the two who are one are better off as each one does their part for the other. "In all the nuts and bolts of domestic life ... time and energy ... caring for and nurturing each other."

So if I am not fully committed to marriage as my priority, who will love, date, romance, pursue, protect, flirt with, be physical with, go out of their way for, build up, encourage, listen to, and be friends with my spouse? Likewise, if she does not view our marriage as important, what about me? We are both, then, left wanting. Yes, because the same way we were made to walk with God, we are also made, for this time that we are here on earth, to walk with one another.

Herein lies the problem. So many couples, as long as they are still together and the principles of marriage are loosely pursued, usually when one is absolutely drained or has felt less than for months, maybe even years, when they finally let it all out, the other spouse might recommit their efforts to the actual person-to-person part of the marriage temporarily. But how sad!

Do you think that our soccer player friend would still be on the team if, after he had made all of the effort in the practices, was lackluster in his actual game performance when it counted most?

Would that worker, who was front and center to all the trainings, showing up on time and working his heart out all day till the closing bell rang, still have his job if, after the store doors opened for the first time, he was nowhere to be found but looking at his watch waiting for his ride home to arrive?

No, because the nuts and bolts needed to hold those standards fell off long ago. The nurture and care couldn't care less any more.

What's happens then in marriage is when our spouse is not priority, we begin to take one another for granted. And in order to sustain our appearance of effort, we default to manipulation or even possibly deceit.

I say this here and now as a severe caution. This may be where your marriage began to take a wrong turn some time ago. We begin to put our spouse on the back burner, and our friends give us more satisfaction. Suddenly the Internet, shopping, or the gym begins to be what satisfies us; and before long we are making up reasons to get on with our own life rather than including our spouse or making the time. But why? Because there is a pain and a void, something that isn't being fulfilled and something that is meant, when pertaining to marriage, to be only between you and your spouse.

Even while writing this, I can hear my wife counseling a struggling spouse on the phone who is fighting for her marriage while the husband is out and about every night, saying he's with friends, making excuses to not hang out, and becoming manipulative in language. She's made to feel as if it's her fault for fighting for this.

"There is no love between us …"

"Things changed long ago …"

"We are different people now …"

Crazy that all of this is without godly perspective, not led of the Spirit, and taking this couple even closer to divorce.

As she asks sensitive questions about his walk, his response is one of defense and "who are you to judge me?" As their future looks bleak and he opts out of any responsibility to their marriage, she is told that the pain she is feeling isn't fair to put on him, and that he's got a plan to work this all out which will allow both of them to get on with their lives, separately, regardless of the children.

What needs to happen is he needs to be sat down, told that as all of his friends are running around flirting with everyone, jumping into bed with different women every week, and painting a merry picture of the life he could be living, he is more distant from God than he has ever been. He is not listening to God's voice but another's, and his daily life has now become one of deceiving others because he himself has been deceived, as his marriage before God is no longer a priority.

Where he is, and where you may be as well, is on your way out of what God has planned for you, and you are looking more like a spouse in the world than one in the kingdom.

As we hear about this common situation, to be more personal, where are you two in your relationship? Is it filled with honesty or manipulation, or even guilt-tripping to get your own way?

I can say this because when Tracy and I went through our divorce, we never made the effort to outright lie to one another, but we bought the lie that we simply needed to survive. So we made sure we ourselves were happy and would make it through the pain of divorce and separation. We would, as needed, not be open about everything we were doing. We would hide our hearts' intentions and focus far more on other things, as it was truly more difficult to stop, go to God (because we weren't saved), and put all of our emotions, pains, and hurts before Him to handle.

These final ten chapters are about much more personal details within our marriages and the things we as humans tend to fall into and use to protect our hearts.

Today, you need to know a few things. Because it is God's will for your marriage to work, as you both seek His will for yourself and one another, know that any kind of deception, dishonesty, and withholding truth will do nothing for your future.

Tonight would be a good time to personally sit and meditate on your walk, your marriage, and ask God how you may be being led toward ungodly ways or people other than your spouse, even though you think nothing will happen. It might even be family members or friends you confide in as a way to express your anger at your spouse. Maybe situations where you don't give your all to rebuilding the bridge of trust, communication, and unity because it's easier to be satisfied elsewhere.

Your goal in prayer is to ask God: Is my marriage my priority, or am I simply just maintaining a marriage by the world's principles?

Search me, God, and know my heart; test me and know my anxious thoughts. See if there is any offensive way in me, and lead me in the way everlasting.

Psalm 139:23–24

DAY 23: LAY ASIDE EVERY WEIGHT

I never looked at it this way. I mean, we come to Christ, so "The old has gone, the new is here!" (2 Corinthians 5:17). Isn't it just that easy? Yes, it is spiritually: Christ died for you, then you repented and received His forgiveness, you became born again, and biblical terminology tells us you were saved, are being saved, and are going to be saved.

So what have we to stress about if everything has been handled? Well, though Christ did everything by His perfect blood offering in our place, we ourselves are still the ones waking up daily to live every breath on mission.

So picture this, if you would. Using one of your favorite songs, "Jesus Take the Wheel," by Carrie Underwood as an example, your life before Christ is all over the place. We are slaves to sin and we are on our so-called jolly way crashing into everything in sight, causing more and more damage as we go.

Then suddenly and out of nowhere, Jesus shows up, taking the wheel and redirecting our lives. Not only does He take the wheel, but the whole car. Not only does He take the car, but He also gives us a map, the Bible, for us to follow to make sure we have directions. And as we continue the struggle, not only do we have directions, but we also have an inner GPS system, the Holy Spirit, who leads and directs as we listen for His voice at every stop sign, side road, and obstacle we encounter. If this isn't enough, He goes all the more out of His way for us and even fits our car with all the safety bags we need, making sure that "no weapon formed against" us spiritually will prosper (Isaiah 54:17, NKJV).

I'd say Jesus has done everything He could have done, but He even goes a step further. He is also the one who built the car, fills it with oil, starts the engine, takes it in for repairs, and is ready at the finish line, waving flag and all, as we finish our race.

With this metaphor in mind, why is it that after we come to faith and begin our walks with Jesus, amazed that He died for us and beginning to receive all of His promises and direction, that as our cars begin down the path of life He has given us, we begin to fill our windshield with baggage, thereby blocking our view and causing both where we are going and how we are responding to our Lord's leading to be as though we are on a permanent roundabout? Yes, one of those weird round English things that we go around and around looking for the right sign, hoping to make our exit onto our final destination.

Well, have you ever tried driving with luggage all over your lap? How about a window filled with old smelly laundry? You'll find that your driving isn't as accurate, it's hindered, and you end up in a canal or even through a store window.

Some years ago, as I was about to head into a particularly difficult time in my life, I was asking the Lord why so many people come to faith excited, motivated, and eager to hear nothing but the voice of the Lord yet they are suddenly bombarded and distracted. What is it that causes them to lose their pace or look as though their very car, if we can continue with the metaphor, is broken down, out of gas, and with flat tires?

It was in prayer that a powerful verse from Hebrews came to mind: "Let us also lay aside every weight …" (Hebrews 12:1, esv).

"Lay aside every weight"? Didn't we do that at salvation? Hasn't the windshield been cleared so we can now see clearly? Yes, we once were blind but now we see. We were lost but now are found.

The verse goes on to say: "Let us also lay aside every weight, and sin which clings so closely" (Hebrews 12:1, esv). Upon taking a closer look at this verse, we see that the *weight* spoken of is something separate than sin, and that we are to let go of both of these things daily. We always focus on the sin mentioned in this verse but what is this "weight," and why are we to lay it aside?

In the Greek, we see the transliteration *ogkos* pinpoints more accurately that this word "weight" means whatever "bulk, mass, burden, encumbrance" that may be in our way, hindering our progress.

As 2012 began, I was about to head into one of the toughest years of my life. This verse being heavy on my heart was no coincidence. My mother, who had battled cancer for two years, succumbed to its deadly bite as I sat bedside her with our family in Liverpool, and she graduated from here into eternity. My wife, almost five month's pregnant, after seeing sonograms and naming our unborn daughter, miscarried and entered into a strenuous season of anxiety. Yes, we had been divorced, met Jesus, and been remarried, but here were new challenges, things outside of the lives we had been living, suddenly facing loved ones passing away and emotions that shook us to the very core. And yes, it hurt!

How would our days look? Thoughts were everywhere and in that season where would we focus? Well, what does God's Word say? "Lay aside every weight"? Was my mother's passing and my wife's miscarriage just some weight? No, our experiences were traumatic and new to our little family, but as I stepped back, even flying home the day after my mother's passing, while on the plane almost numb to what was going on around me, what did I know? *Lay aside the weight.*

Was my car about to be all over the road? Was my wife going to put her car in park and not even look to Jesus who had taken the wheel? No, we carried on and we pressed in, even to the point where the night after I got home, I preached a message at Calvary Chapel Pacific Coast on, yes, laying aside your weight.

You see, after coming through that season, that word helped me to see that daily, with every breath, if I am really to live on purpose, I am going to have to learn to put things in perspective, try to see them God's way, and keep pressing in.

With this in mind, I can now look back at that difficult year saying the only thing I can be bummed about is that I didn't get to meet my daughter before my mother did. You see, because my mother confessed Jesus as Lord on her deathbed, and because my unborn child would have gone to be with the Lord, my hope today is that they are very much acquainted and spending plenty of time together in heaven.

And when we look at our marriages and purposely lay aside our weights and struggles, our journey is going to make more sense and be all the more smooth.

To picture this idea even more, revisit with me the famed *A Christmas Carol* by Charles Dickens (the 1970 Albert Finney movie version, of course). As the film begins we are introduced to our man, Ebenezer Scrooge, who, now well into the later years of his life, has nothing good to say, is bitter, has no close friends, and even at Christmastime greets every pleasant comment with a "bah humbug." What is his problem? Why is he mad? What is he holding onto?

As he returns home one night, sitting before his fireplace warming himself because of the winter weather, we hear a voice calling out to him from the dark.

"Scrooooooge, Scrooooooge!!!" numerous times as we see Scrooge trying to figure out and understand what is happening. His deceased friend, Jacob Marley, enters through a wall as a spirit to which Scrooge in his stubbornness and hardness of heart tells him "you're an hallucination probably brought on by an … old potato. Yes, that's what you are; you are an old potato!"

But as Marley begins to bang the chains together that are surrounding and attached to him, Scrooge asks, "What is that great chain you wear"? And Jacob's response is astonishing, "I wear the chain I forged in life, I made it link by link and yard by yard while on earth, and now I'll never be rid of it any more than you will ever be rid of yours!"[1]

He explains to Scrooge that the very life he is living is forging for him in death a chain he will carry for eternity. Every encounter, deed, and response has bent him toward heading into an eternity that represents his heart.

Suddenly, we are taken on a journey to view the story of Scrooge's life, back into the past where we see a happy and joyful young man enjoying family, friends, a girlfriend, and a life that could have been. But as life unfolds, challenges come, loved ones pass, relationships are broken, and soon wounds that cut deep transform him into someone far from whom he once was.

Fortunately for Scrooge, as he grasps what lays before him and the path that he is on, he awakens from this dream, it's Christmas morning, and he is eager to make the necessary changes in his life to go out and live a life of purpose: One that doesn't involve the past but the plan for the future.

What a story, one where his car seemed broken down, his tires were flat, and he swayed far from the road he had once set out upon. Just as we, in the midst of our marriages and our relationships with Jesus, can be all over the road because of the weight, baggage, or chains we carry.

So should we, in any way, after having an even deeper revelation than Scrooge, seeing that we once carried chains but now have passed from "death to life" (1 John 3:14) and have been "hidden with Christ" (Colossians 3:3) resemble this Christmas classic at all?

Should my walk be all over the place when the God I serve and who died for me has called me to "lay aside every weight"?

The obvious answer is no, and we see the reason in the next part of verse 1. We are called to lay aside the weight that we might "run with endurance the race that is set before us" (Hebrews 12:1, ESV).

---

[1] *Scrooge.* Dir. Ronald Neame. Perf. Albert Finney, Alec Guinness. Paramount, 2003. DVD.

The race is set before us, we need endurance, and today is the day you take these past twenty-two chapters of this book and "lay aside the weight."

Extra weight is something we don't want to carry. As a skateboarder, for years traveling the world, there was one thing I didn't like to take with me: weight, baggage, and luggage. As we would head out on skate trips, going to the airport, there would always be one team rider with all the skateboards, trucks, wheels, DVDS, movies, bags, etc. He was the one late to the airport, late on the plane, late off the plane, late to the hotel, late out of the hotel, and late to skate. He was slowing himself down, but everyone else as well. Weight will do that, and the author of Hebrews is telling us to let go of the weight as we run this race because it will only hinder.

The apostle Paul also presents our walk as a race, not against others, but one that is actually our own—one we are to focus on. People of that day and age would have understood his athletic references completely, as physical competition was huge in that day.

> Do you not know that those who run in a race all run, but one receives the prize? Run in such a way that you may obtain it.
>
> *1 Corinthians 9:24, NKJV*

> An athlete is not crowned unless he competes according to the rules.
>
> *2 Timothy 2:5, ESV*

To "run in such a way" and "according to the rules." Well, along with having no others gods before God and loving our neighbor as ourselves, being filled with the Spirit, living out the Great Commission, and making disciples, it is evident we are also to "lay aside every weight."

As you consider this today, as we finish up this chapter, what weights are you still holding on to? You see, this world has influenced us in so many ways; we hold on to the past and respond out of how those things made us feel.

Coming from Liverpool, England, I constantly got into fights. This *weight* would come out in my marriage as Tracy and I began to fight. I carried this baggage, I was not letting go of it, and I was possibly even the one who packed it. See, you don't know what is inside my baggage, my luggage, my weight. Only Jesus does, and He died to free me from it. And though it has my name and address on it, now *I* need to lay it aside because throughout Scripture, we see how weights have played a deadly part in leading many people astray.

Why did Cain kill Abel (Genesis 4)? Yes, out of jealousy, but wouldn't you say that was his baggage? He could have laid it aside?

Why did King Saul want to kill David? Because the Bible tells us Saul "kept a close eye on David" (1 Samuel 18:9). He was jealous because the people favored David.

If we don't let go of the weight, it will not only hinder us, but it will spill over to affect our family, our homes, our children, our very lives.

There's no better picture of this than the one we are about to look at. In Luke's gospel, we see Jesus approaching the home of two sisters. Picture with me Jesus walking up to your home today. You and your spouse are inside, and you hear a knock on the door. Wow! The architect of the universe, the one who would die for your sins, the one who loves you with perfect love and who is the one in which all life is found has arrived.

As you open the door and He enters, how do you react? We read that as He entered Martha's home, "she had a sister called Mary, who also sat at Jesus' feet and heard His word. But Martha was distracted with *much* serving, and she approached Him and said, '*Lord*, do You not care that my sister has left me to serve alone? Therefore tell her to help me" (Luke 10:39–42, NKJV, emphasis mine).

This is a familiar story, but an often overlooked and easily missed picture is found herein. Jesus, the Savior of mankind, enters a home where one sister falls at His feet to hear "His word." But Martha, the other sister "was distracted with much serving." Not only is she distracted, she approaches Him and rudely challenges Him, asking if He cares that Mary has left her to serve alone. Then, as if this wasn't ridiculous enough, she tells Him what to do, "tell her to help me."

As I sit here letting this picture play out in my mind, I can't imagine myself missing Jesus, not falling to His feet, and awaiting what it is He has to say. But as I look at myself more closely, how often do I instead run about busy, with my mind elsewhere, thinking everything I am doing is in His Name? It's interesting—when we look at this passage, we see that Martha actually calls Jesus "Lord." She understood who He was, but her mind and focus was far from Him.

I ask you today: which sibling would you be in this story—the one falling at His feet, or the one trying to call the shots, running about busy, missing what He has to say even while calling Him Lord?

Before you answer, consider that word *distracted*: too busy over something, drawn away, to be driven about mentally, or even overly occupied.

Is that you? Are you in the midst of your relationship with Jesus, preoccupied with what your boss may do, how to get your life up to that standard society projects, still hurt over what may have happened to you years ago, or unable to forgive others for something they once did to you?

When we are distracted, we, like Martha, miss the very person who is most important—Jesus!

Jesus, being aware of what's happening, answers Martha, saying, "Martha, Martha, you are worried and troubled about many things" (Luke 10:41, NKJV). As plain as day, His goal is to stop her in her tracks and correct her perspective, get the car back on the right path, break away some chains, and lay aside the weight. I love that He says her name twice, "Martha, Martha," which in the original language is both a urgent address and the voice of a loving parent. He continues and goes on to tell this daughter of God, "you are worried and troubled about many things."

Not only does He address the issue but He gives the solution, one which we must take heed to today.

"But one thing is needed, and Mary has chosen that good part, which will not be taken away from her."

Luke 10:42, NKJV

"One thing is needed," and it is something that Mary chose. Are you following here? We began in Hebrews with this command: "let us lay aside every weight," the "us" part meaning something *we do*. Yes, He has already done it; He accomplished all that was needed on the cross. But we, you and I, need to be the ones who choose to "lay aside every weight," just as Mary chose the "one thing" that was needed—to fall at her Master's feet in worship to hear, to fellowship, to be weight free.

By now, day twenty-three, we should have felt the road He has set before us, the race we are in, the freedom of walking in Christ. Yes, it's a battle but it's one He has already won and one that we need to exercise our faith in, as we do the very things He has called us to do.

Right now, in your marriage, wouldn't your future look better by setting aside any lingering weights, any dated luggage, and any rusting chains of bondage?

As we run with endurance the race set before us, whatever those weights may be, we overcome them and their hold on us as we look "to Jesus, the founder and perfecter of our faith" (Hebrews 12:2, ESV).

When was the last time you looked unto Jesus? Is He before you today, but your knee deep in distractions and need to release what's bound inside? Like the women with the issue of blood for twelve years, she reached out to touch Jesus' garment and was healed (see Mark 5). Jesus, knowing this, cried out to see who touched Him and why His power had gone out. He knew who she was, of course, but He was calling for her to respond. Why? So He could bless her, call her His daughter, and send her in peace. She received these things because she came and fell down in worship before Him, "looking to" Him.

We read in Mark's gospel about the man who was demonized and tormented by demons that "When he saw Jesus from afar, he ran and worshiped Him" (Mark 5:6, NKJV).

See the difference from where you are in life and consider previous examples. I was once controlled by anger; Scrooge was to be bound by chains; Martha was distracted, worn, and frustrated; a woman was plagued with an issue of blood for twelve years; a demoniac was tormented and enslaved. All of these things can be addressed when we fall at the feet of Jesus, release the weight, let go of the baggage, and clear the windshield of our lives.

As we close up this chapter (and I apologize for it being one of the longest ones), why not spend some time praying through what may come to mind that is hindering your focus and your view, that which has kept you circling the roundabout of life that Jesus has set you free from.

He said, "My yoke is easy and my burden is light" (Matthew 11:30), so should we not, in faith, choose to let go of any weight?

If possible, pray together, forgiving one another and forgetting, and release any weight that God brings to mind.

DAY 24: FOXES IN THE VINEYARDS

Of all the things we can bring up (character flaws, pet peeves, issues, problems, differences, disagreements, fights, lack of love, and so on) for why our marriages struggle and hurt, is there really anything more dangerous than lust and adultery?

How many marriages were built on solid ground yet suddenly were shattered after flirtation, lust, and adultery showed up. We push back right away on the thought that "it would never happen to us;" "we are madly in love;" "there will never be anyone else for me!" But when we do that, we are missing the problem. The problem isn't just in other people; it is in us, part of our nature, both yours and mine, no matter how Ned Flanders your marriage may be.

It's one thing to blame Satan for sin, but what about actually looking within and holding ourselves accountable? I sat with a couple this past week whose marriage I will have the privilege of officiating in the near future. Amidst the glances, smiles, hand holding, and even kisses as they picture their marriage day—the dress, the hair, the flowers, the beauty, the photography, the home, the romance, the sex, the family, and the future—I stopped them mid-conversation to challenge their vision and to make them aware of what lies ahead. I am well aware of the beauty of what God is shaping in them, yet I had only just got off the phone from talking to a housewife whose family, only a few years in the making, has been shattered because of her husband's infidelity.

When they had planned their marriage, were they simply looking to the positives and the goals driven by culture while turning a blind eye to one another's very nature? And yes, I mean sin nature.

When God tells us in Genesis 4:7 that "sin is crouching," He means it. And it is not that sin is outside of ourselves and it leads us; no, sin is within, and the things we encounter stroke and speak to it. In fact "… each person is tempted when they are dragged away by their own evil desire and enticed. Then, after desire has conceived, it gives birth to sin; and sin, when it is full-grown, gives birth to death" (James 1:14–16).

So to tackle this issue head-on. Every person is tempted when they give in to their own evil desire. As this desire leads us, we submit to its ways, and before you know it, ideas and possibilities are laid out and death becomes a reality.

Here we are blaming what is on the outside, what enters our body—the temple—daily through screen, audio, and interaction. But no matter the format, the issue lies within, and just so you know, this will happen until death.

Because of this truth, let me ask you, how solid is your marriage? How airtight are the possibilities for the enemy to tempt, for you to get as close to sin without doing it, for the enemy to reveal to you what's in your heart, making you step into his playground without perhaps sticking around?

If you can, picture your marriage as an estate. Your home is in the middle, and your vineyards carry on to the edge roads or the coast. There in the midst, you and your spouse are enjoying life, romancing one another, honoring your vows without distraction, and not thinking of greener grasses. Even when times are tough, the voice you are hearing is the Lord's, both by His Word and the encouragement of your spouse.

Suddenly out of nowhere, as love is all around, your attention is drawn away, as you find the seeds you had sown for your family's future harvest torn apart and scattered all over your property.

Days go by, and you can't quite figure out what is happening or why what was once flourishing is losing both its color and taste. Your focus is gone, days run long, but after an exhaustive season, you finally figure it out.

Hiring the most Rambo version of a gardener/hunter/exterminator you can find, you give him only one goal: "Catch for us the foxes, the little foxes that ruin the vineyards, our vineyards that are in bloom" (Song of Solomon 2:15).

Yes, as beautiful as your estate may be, foxes pursue it with the aim to ruin your vineyards, eventually dividing the estate. Where do these foxes come from, how do they sneak in and are they sometimes even invited?

Well, if we just stop for a moment and consider our idea of marriage, how within that estate do you view the amount of opposite-sex friends you should have? What place and importance do your relationships from the past have? What about the new ones you will develop through work, sports, social media, and yes, even church?

This past week, I sat in an accountability session with a man who has been married almost half of his life; he had only just confessed that day of his recent infidelity to his wife. It's been a few days now and the family is devastated. His wife doesn't know what she will do; the kids, who are in their early twenties, are beside themselves with anger trying to figure out who dad is and where the man they once knew went; and he himself is as broken as can be.

It was a friendship that had bloomed over time, a fellow worker who, bit by bit, became a fox who entered the vineyard. Perhaps it was how much nicer than his wife she was that day, the outfit she wore, the way her hair looked as she dressed to exhibit herself. Maybe it was the business texts or the online media as they relayed simple thoughts, messages that gradually made way for the sin nature abiding in us all. Undoubtedly the pictures and visions that went around their heads have been fueled by the almost porn-like society we live in now where movie screens, feature films, TV soaps, award ceremonies, and books speak of affairs and one-night stands as if we should expect them.

Sadly, the lesson learned here, as hopefully they make it through this season, is that it's long been time to keep those foxes out of your vineyards and away from your estate.

There's a reason my wife and I have access to everything we are engaged in. Our phones, texts, emails, Facebook pages, Instagram, Twitters (and whatever else may be on the horizon) are mutually ours and mutually a platform of accountability.

We have had a crazy marriage, one that ended in divorce and was resurrected by Christ when we came to faith, but one that nonetheless needs all the accountability it can get.

Since we are now one, why would I want it any other way? If sin is crouching, don't I want my best friend to help fend off anything that tries to sneak its way in? Not only do I want this, but this is how God intended it.

And when we live like this, it keeps us humble, dependent on His plan, and also openly repentant.

See, the world builds a presentation for us as to what we like, yet it is God who defines this by simply giving us a spouse. They are our standard and preference, and God is not wrong.

This is why I don't need to have women who are best friends the way I once did, who were as close as could be without being physical, which, before Christ, may well have been exactly where we ended up.

This is why every email, message, text, or phone call is available to my wife and I so as to not make any room for the enemy. Are you actually aware of the statistics showing that most affairs begin online, and even if it never becomes physical or even emotional, why are we fishing through someone else's photos and life while we already have a spouse to be occupied with?

It would be smart for all of us as believers to reword the questions we ask ourselves, as we keep ourselves in check. It's not: have I looked at porn, but have I lusted after a woman?

Is it going to help my marriage if my wife begins to notice every handsome actor, crude vampire film, or movie about seduction? While people joke and post man-crush Mondays or check out whoever is half naked across our supermarket shelves, is this not pushing us more toward tasting of another fruit, laying down in other pastures, and more importantly living in opposition to God's Word?

Sadly, these boundaries are rarely set within relationships because they seem so extreme … until things have gone too far. Recently I've been counseling a couple that have been working through an affair. During our sessions, the wife would always refer to how the husband was "like a Nazi," and how he always wanted to set boundaries and bring things into the light. While he himself did have some of his own foxes entering the vineyards, I had to stop them both to address this: "Could it be that the boundaries he was eager to set may well have been the reason why he was not the one living in infidelity?"

To not consider how important it is to set boundaries and be accountable is to miss the selfishness of both our need to be wanted and the wickedness of our sinful nature.

I cannot count how many times I have told people to erase numbers from their phones, cut off ties to past relationships, and open up your current interactions with everyone else to your spouse.

If my wife and I were not believers, how would we be living in this world? Would she be out pursuing the dream career, wearing low-cut tops and skin-tight clothes while participating in what's the norm in society, making herself something to be desired, wanted, lusted after, and eventually pursued?

Would she have come into contact with a good friend from school that she never stayed connected with but at one time there was a bond or attraction established?

Suddenly, he is in town; he's looked her up online. She's already flattered he thought of her, but our relationship is solid, so it's simply meeting for coffee and catching up.

As they meet, "it's so good to see you," and they speak of how things are going in their lives. He doesn't complain like I do, doesn't tell her how to spend our money, but instead he sits and listens, compliments her recent haircut, comments on how great she looks now, and surely, he notices her behind.

The stage has already been set. We have seen it over and over; we know where this can end up … the only difference now is, do we want the foxes out of the vineyards? Did we forget the estate we established, the land we thanked the Lord for, and the promises we entered into and asked God to bless?

You will find yourself returning again and again to these kinds of interactions with people you find attractive, who flatter you, or who add superficially to your worth. It's our sin nature. Aren't people already dressing up to stand out, to be noticed, to live above the rest?

You have to ask yourselves today, "Do we understand this? Have we seen marriages destroyed because couples didn't pursue godly lives and protect their borders?

Keep in mind, this is not about control; it's about safety. It's not about fear; it really is about faith. Do you believe this is how God would want us to protect one another? I don't know the boundaries you need to set, but I have friends who have walked through every extreme to protect their marriages.

Televisions taken out of hotel rooms, passwords on their computers, not going to the gym alone; yes, everyone is on display. Not driving in the car with a woman alone. Cutting off ties to conversations outside of what's necessary.

Even sitting here and writing this, it sounds like a list of do's and don'ts. Please don't view it that way. Understand, we are entering this chapter with the goal of sustaining our marriages and being aware of both the enemy's attacks and our own weaknesses.

No one is above this but God. And He told us through the words of Solomon: "Above all else, guard your heart, for everything you do flows from it. Keep your mouth free of perversity; keep corrupt talk far from your lips. Let your eyes look straight ahead; fix your gaze directly before you. Give careful thought to the paths for your feet and be steadfast in all your ways. Do not turn to the right or the left; keep your foot from evil" (Proverbs 4:23–27).

He instructs to make no room "for the flesh" (Romans 13:14, ESV); but what greater way to do so than opening ourselves to flirtation and lust, which sadly leads to adultery?

It sounds so foreign because crushes and relating are such a part of our culture, but it's more than likely that even while reading this chapter, the Lord has already shown ways to make your relationship airtight.

Because this is something you both will need to step into, this is not a time to get defensive or argumentative. This is a time to stop and consider. Rather than bring up people or past situations, first simply go to the Lord, asking Him to reveal to us anyone we may have been closer with than is best, even if it was innocent, and also to consider possible ways in which we walk and interact with others that we know are not from God.

If you want to face this head-on, ask how you may well act with others when your spouse is not around.

Spend some time praying through this, and then, with the goal of keeping the foxes out of your vineyard, mutually begin to establish boundaries. You will probably have a different gauge on where these boundaries are, and even this can be frustrating. But if you are really in it, for this marriage, and most importantly for God, then you will be eager to listen to your spouse, not just to hear their boundaries but hear their concerns and their heart. As time goes on, you will see where boundaries may be adjusted and situations will be handled all the more with the focus on protecting your estate.

In a nutshell, do you want to commit adultery against God? Are we not here to love others, respect others, and stay out of their vineyards while keeping others out of our own? Life is about Christ and our testimony for Him.

For some of you, this has been a tough chapter. To hear God's heart on this, dig into Proverbs 5, 6, and 7. These will surely help you to understand the depth of the sin of adultery. It is, after all, the only sin by which one is allowed to divorce.

DAY 25: ROMANCING YOUR SPOUSE

It is strange … I can't exactly explain it … almost magnetic or like gravity. Literally, as the head of the house and the man in the relationship, I can't think of anything that makes my days more of a struggle than to be distant from my wife. Equally, I can't think of anyone who is able to give me the comfort and security in almost any situation than her. It was these feelings and bonds that took place when we first courted, as we got more and more doses of one another, found one another's rhythms, and catered to one another's needs.

This Monday marks our fifteen-year anniversary, and I am still beside myself thinking of what to do to make my wife feel special and to "honor," her as the Bible tells me.

Does she know I love her? Of course! Does she know our future is secured? Yes! And it is because of this that I make the point to pursue and romance her every opportunity I can. Likewise, I look forward to the effort she puts forth in making my relevance and her love for me equally known.

Sadly, as marriage goes on and we jump through difficult hoops, we can become so hard-hearted to one another that the closeness we once pursued is sacrificed. We once forsook so many things to pursue our spouses, yet we can easily find ourselves forsaking our spouse for other things now. Is this not so true?

With three kids and my dad currently on vacation living with us, Tracy and I have had barely any time together, but even tonight, as we headed out to meet an engaged couple, raining and all, the time alone on the journey there and back refueled us from any of the week's meltdowns, blowouts, or conflicts.

Because God is good, is for our marriage, and views my wife and I as one, I have to live my days aware that the more on the same page we are, the more fluid our days are going to be. The magnetism or gravity I spoke of earlier in the chapter is best explained in Genesis chapter 2:18, where God says, "It is not good for the man to be alone." Solomon later said, "He who finds a wife finds a good thing" (Proverbs 18:22, ESV).

How do I live a life not feeling alone, the opposite of many couples who live under the same roof while feeling the loneliest they possibly could? The answer has to be romance. Putting in the time and living as if we were first dating. Couples can become so like roommates, still doing things together, building memories, even being physical, while having lost the passion and bond they once had.

Romance is the solution to this, and is evidently the only way to keep one another aware of the other's interest. Don't get me wrong—we can say we love and do things that the world would say are loving, but the romance part between a loving couple will only echo deeper the waves of love within us.

By definition, romance is the feeling of excitement, the mystery surrounding our love, and what is acted out as we woo and court one another.

Why would we want our days and interactions with our spouse any other way, especially because of all we will face?

I've noticed that within marriages, especially secular ones and those outside the faith, it is when the feeling of romance has gone that they begin to look the other way, need to find excitement elsewhere, and not only say, but even believe that they have fallen out of love. Applying this to our biblical perspective simply means we are not doing the exciting things we once did, not making the time for one another to feel special, and not going out of our way to stir one another up.

Today, if we could ask God for wisdom on the matter of romance, He would surely lead us to these words: "Let your fountain be blessed, and rejoice in the wife of your youth, a lovely deer, a graceful doe" (Proverbs 5:18–19, ESV).

How can I possibly rejoice in Tracy, the wife of my youth, if I don't carry the same feelings and emotions we built into our relationship during our youth? We may not be spending all of our time driving to and from LA, eating at vegan restaurants, seeing bands play, going around the world with my skate career, or spinning around the teacups at Disneyland (wow, they make my head hurt now). But here she is, 37 years of age, about to celebrate fifteen years of marriage, divorced from me once, married me twice, has given birth to our three children, has been there through the hardest times in my life, surely has grey hairs on the horizon, and is still walking this crazy life we live as Christians.

Now, I don't know about you, but if I can't find something exciting, interesting, and magical within our marriage and memories to draw emotion for the path we are still on, then I have to question, what was it that died in me?

If you are here in the midst of this book aiming to further your marriage, then "Let love be your greatest aim" (1 Corinthians 14:1, TLB). Aim at the wife of your youth. As I look toward what my wife may possibly be expecting December 8th, do I have the Holy Spirit within me to help as I plan things simply for her, as she in turn, is hopefully planning for me?

For us personally, we as a couple don't want or need all the bells and whistles. I am not impressed by money spent on things that may say an awful lot until they rust or tear. For us, it is more about being present, doing something that creates new memories, and also assures us that we made it through another year and are both on board to keep the flame alive for as many years as remain.

Because romance is something personal to you both as a couple, you two are the ones who walked out the season of bonding that first brought you together.

Though you were in a different place when you first met, perhaps in your walk or even before facing the difficulties as you grew and were shaped in marriage, you both have to know and believe today that if you begin to pay enough attention to one another and the "race set before" you, you will bond and connect, finding things that will once again bring your marriage back into the center of your lives.

Whether it is your anniversary or not, what would it look like if you took the next week to purposely go out of your way to pursue your spouse? What if you knew you only had one week left with that person, and this was all the time you had to show them how much they mean to you. What would you do?

Now to bring you into my world, what am I going to do for my wife? The television screams of expensive jewelry, how a woman loves diamonds, yet she just doesn't care for jewelry. Maybe invest some of our finances, or if I have enough air miles, what about a romantic trip to Hawaii (the Pipeline Pro is in December, after all)? Yet my wife, she does not like to fly, so what do I do?

Well, what I know of my wife, even though she may not realize it, is she likes to be confirmed as my wife and as a mother—the things God has created her to be. She also likes to eat healthy, and whenever we are out, whether it is in the store or around friends, she is talking about ingredients, cooking, and what's good for you. Also she likes garage sales, finding vintage things and old furniture.

If you were me, what would you do for your 15th anniversary? Well, of all the things I can plan, what I did was, I asked her!

Her response was quite a surprise. "Let's just go Christmas shopping." Really? That was her plan? Well, she had been busy running all over the place and had not had time to rest.

This could be a night of playlists of the songs we fell in love to, an absence of three screaming kids (or just kids in general), eating uninterrupted at her favorite place, getting ahead as we enter into this busy season, and most importantly for us, simply time alone. This, along with a trip to Anthropology and some other things I wanted to bless her with, made a simple evening romantic.

And that is just how it went. For our anniversary, for it to be romantic, all we did was listen to what one the other wanted. We made time and gave of ourselves for the other, just like when we first met and grew together.

In all honesty, looking forward in your marriage, make the time to hear one another, be available, and give of yourself. This in turn will maintain and stir up the love you first felt.

Being equally as honest, letting these things go dormant will only silence the voice of love within your marriage, and the excitement, magnetism, and feelings of being wooed you once felt will be void.

Are you ready to revisit and speak into the romance you once felt? Is there pride or hurt that has gotten in the way? What better time than now to exercise your faith and trust in the things of God as you love on the spouse He has given you?

Choose today to move forward and walk in the romance He has for you as you pursue your spouse in love.

Let us not love with words or speech but with actions and in truth.

1 John 3:18

Let all that you do be done in love.

1 Corinthians 16:14, ESV

DAY 26: SEX!

What about it? Dare we mention it? Does your pastor speak of it? Are people uncomfortable if the topic comes up? Is it really that big of a deal or that important within our marriages? We could go on all day about sex. In fact, isn't it well said, "sex sells"? Best-selling books, edgy movies, and culture is pushing the idea that being "sexy" is something to be desired, strived for, and the norm.

We don't even have to establish how important sex is. Anyone hitting their mid-teens can probably tell you that the porn industry generates billions of dollars a year as it floods homes through the lenses of computer screens, cell phones, and other forms of technology.

So sex needs to be addressed, especially when within the church it is often presented as too taboo to talk about. But when considering this topic and seeing how many people within my own life, both in and out of the faith, have wide and vastly different concepts, I have to consider how my own children are going to understand sex. Where will they learn of it? Will they understand it to be a curse, taboo, or a blessing from God?

My fourteen-year-old son has been playing baseball for many years. And I am well aware that most of what he has heard about sex has been in the dugout from the mouths of teenagers. Sadly, much of what has shaped his understanding of sex has come from sources outside of the Bible. See, for my son, for myself at his age, and for you, sex has been a major part of our thought processes since we first heard about it. Just the other night, my wife had just sat down beside me on our couch, turned the channel to ABC Family, and Rock of Ages was playing on the screen. Here comes Tom Cruise exiting a room after getting sexy and lewd with a reporter. Where's the remote?! CLICK!

In our world, sex is all around us. And because of the emotions, passions, and desires it arouses, we need to establish early on that sex is both a gift from God, but it is also a weapon of the enemy when abused.

To begin, though the church for years didn't know how to handle it, talk about, and even forbade it at certain times, do we not first hear of sex from God Himself? In Genesis 1:28, He tells Adam and Eve to "be fruitful and multiply" (ESV). Wow! Who would have thought that the God we serve told married couples to have sex? Would anyone be here if they had not taken up this command? And because God said this, wouldn't it be considered sin to not "be fruitful and multiply"?

God introduced sex, and consider that this command came before the curse, before man fell.

God blessed them and said to them, "Be fruitful and [multiply]."

Genesis 1:28

We see in this verse that sex is a blessing *from God*, a gift, something to be enjoyed between a man and his wife.

"Therefore a man shall leave his father and his mother and hold fast to his wife, and they shall become one flesh. And the man and his wife were both naked and were not ashamed."

Genesis 2:24–25, ESV

Two people leave their parents and step out into marriage; vows are read, rings are worn. And for the couple who come together as virgins, there is also a shedding of blood, as physically they consummate this holy and sexual union. (I never thought I would be writing such words to couples, but this is God's Word.)

This is what occurred between Adam and Eve. They begin to have children, are fruitful, and they do multiply. And here we see one of God's commands in motion being used for good.

Now, if this could have been how all sex was played out since God first blessed them and introduced it, then the world would be a much different place. But because we have an enemy, the father of lies, we see the results today. Sex is not honored as a gift, but it is instead worshipped and used as a weapon.

In your marriage, do you both have a good understanding of what sex means to your marriage, to one another, and to God? There are many couples today who have never talked with anyone about sex, don't know what to think about it, and who came into a marriage either wounded, feeling ashamed, or embarrassed.

Is it just for making babies; is it only after a romantic evening when it can be truly defined as "making love;" is it a place to live out all of your fantasies?

Where do we go with these thoughts, and what does God really say about sex?

Well, two thousand years ago, while Paul was preaching and starting churches, the believers in Corinth had the same questions in mind. They too had questions about sex as even within their own congregations, sex outside of marriage, orgies, being with prostitutes, and all kinds of sexual rituals to other gods were trying to contaminate God's plans. As Paul responds to the church, he begins by defining clearly that sex is to be between a man and his wife only.

> Now concerning the matters about which you wrote: "It is good for a man not to have sexual relations with a woman." But because of the temptation to sexual immorality, each man should have his own wife and each woman her own husband.
>
> *1 Corinthians 7:1–2, ESV*

Paul tells them it is good not to be sexual with a woman, even saying "because of the temptation to sexual immorality." Meaning what? Because you will be attracted, because you will begin to court, get to know, consider your futures, enjoy her voice, her smell, and your thoughts may even wander, because of this, you should marry, you should have your own wife or, if a woman, your own husband.

I should get married because I want to have sex? No, you should get married because if you continue reading in 1 Corinthians 7, you will see that God gives gifts to people: some not to be married and others to be married. Even Paul himself goes on to talk about him having the gift of singleness. But that means for you, if you are unmarried, or if you think back to when you were first getting to know one another, you were aware that you viewed this person as a possible spouse, that they could be the one, that this could be the person you would be spending your life with, in partnership, and yes, being sexual with. Paul's writing this to say: don't fall into sin; instead, because you feel this way about this person, you should be married.

When you think about how many times a day people are lusting and desiring to be physical with others without the intention of marrying them, you begin to understand how far off we are today from God's plan and how abused sex has become. On God's path, Paul explains, you would only consider being sexual with the person you were growing to know and beginning to have feelings for and praying about marrying. In the same way that he tells such a couple to get married, he is also echoing the text of Song of Solomon 2:7, "Do not arouse or awaken love until it so desires." Do not arouse or awaken this kind of "love." Even within this text, a couple is courting, growing to know one another, and planning toward marriage. But as they do, this Shulamite woman has these thoughts of her spouse-to-be and is charged by her friends to "not arouse or awaken" this kind of love.

If you were to continue reading through Song of Solomon, you would see the marriage unfold and would hear of her husband delighting in her as he pursues her, even saying her "breasts are like two fawns" (4:5, ESV), that she is "altogether beautiful" (4:7), and directly saying of her virginity, "You are a garden locked up, my sister, my bride; you are a spring enclosed, a sealed fountain" (4:12). This type of romantic poetry, tied into the mention of aphrodisiacs, brings us back to the voice of the Shulamite bride who invites her husband to "Awake, north wind, and come, south wind! Blow on my garden, that its fragrance may spread everywhere. Let my beloved come into his garden and taste its choice fruits" (4:16).

When we look at the language of Song of Solomon, we see a couple in love, a romance in bloom, and the highest point uniting all of this is the physical activity set apart only and especially for married couples—sex!

It is not coincidental that children are never mentioned in this book, by the way. So this is straight for their enjoyment and pleasure, to be able to serve one another and further their bond and trust.

In God's eyes, sex, then, is only between husband and wife; any other way is sinful. However, today, sex is cheapened. Most see it as simply getting to know someone, finding them attractive, sharing a few things in common, and something we just do as seen in the movies, magazines, or society. And the world my wife and I grew up in, being non-Christians, we had already been physical with others before marriage. But now, as a pastor, I present sex as what it is: a sacred act. And I've realized that our view of sex isn't the issue but our view of God.

This is why it's important that you, as a couple, put sex back to the position God intends for it to be: set apart, between you and your spouse, something to be cherished and enjoyed.

To be more direct, we live in a culture were men are meant to be more obsessed with sex, which means women are the ones who then control it or use it as a way to manipulate or have power. This idea that a guy will "get some" if the wife feels like it or if he has romanced her enough is a dangerous place to live.

While sitting with couples over this past year, I've noticed that when the wife gets mixed feelings about her husband, she justifies in her head why they no longer will have sex. She makes this conscious decision that she will no longer sleep with him, while she expects him to jump through hoops to prove he is a God-fearing and respectable man, which in turn will flip her sex switch back on.

While it's true that we as men need to love, romance, and pursue our wives, ladies, do you see what's wrong with this picture? The wife has decided to take away one of the foundational parts of what it means to be married, while expecting the guy to be able to function at one hundred percent. This is like taking one of the wheels off of your car and expecting it to drive the same.

Sitting with one couple, I remember asking, "Did God tell you to stop having sex?" to which the woman responded, "I don't feel like it … I just can't right now." But please hear me when I ask, do you see how our whole view of sex is wrong? We have made it something we give or take, meaning it can be manipulated or abused. But sex needs to be something couples do together when it is romantic, when it is not, when it has been a good day or not, when there are no tears, when there are, through victory and even tragedy.

I believe Christians should be having the best sex out there; what do I mean? Just as my communication with Tracy is more open and my commitment to her more solid, so it should be in the sexual realm.

Ladies, I am not saying this to make you think you are just a piece of flesh and your husband can just make demands on that body of yours. Instead I am saying that sex needs to be redefined and understood to build even stronger foundations for your marriages.

Before Tracy and I were believers, when we were facing hard times and going through our divorce, I remember not wanting to be as close physically. I always had mixed emotions, obviously, because I was depressed and over living at that time. Sex was obviously not something I was focused on. If I think of the emotions that it brought out in her, the lack of intimacy she had with me, I would be missing it to not share with you today just how this affects husbands. When you as a spouse switch off physically and view sex as just a physical act, placing it at the bottom of the marital list, it makes it a type of reward. However, when it is seen as intimacy, it becomes an essential foundational factor for the health of your marriage.

Some of the best advice I have given women on the brink of divorce is to go home and begin to be physical with your husband again. It sounds shallow, but when he has had the hardest day, carried the weight of home and finances and self on his shoulders, to simply be able to be enjoyed and enjoy his partner has an effect. *But it's just sex*, you say. Exactly, unless you see it as what it is—a union that bonds, establishes trust, protects, engages, and so much more. Sex in these struggling marriages encourages pursuit of one another, which humbles them; and as they are physical, bonds of trust are built all over again.

The idea of sex being used as a weapon of control among couples is not new. As we continue in Corinthians, Paul addresses husbands and wives, saying: "The husband should give to his wife her conjugal rights, and likewise the wife to her husband. For the wife does not have authority over her own body, but the husband does. Likewise the husband does not have authority over his own body, but the wife does" (1 Corinthians 7:3–4, ESV).

Can you imagine a wife demanding her husband's body, as if she needs to in this day and age? What husband is going to deny his wife that? And even in our thinking, we see the problem. Sex is everywhere, and this is not to justify the sin of pornography, lust, or an affair. But I can tell you, if you starve anyone of anything that God has intended to be a gift, it will cause a person to be off balance and to hunger for what is lacking.

If only women saw their bodies as belonging to their husbands, I can promise you, it would change how much your spouse would even be focused on sex. They would not hunger as much as when starved, as it will be all the more available.

With this in mind, Paul goes on to say:

Do not deprive one another, except perhaps by agreement for a limited time, that you may devote yourselves to prayer; but then come together again, so that Satan may not tempt you because of your lack of self-control.

1 Corinthians 7:5, ESV

We should not deprive one another. We should work to meet one another's sexual needs and balance out within our lives times for intimacy, getting to know one another's bodies again with the goal of serving, pleasuring and, as we see here, protecting. Paul did say not to "deprive one another" unless it's agreed upon for prayer and fasting, but then "come together again" because Satan wants to tempt you through your lack of self-control. Sex, Paul says, is actually a weapon that wars against Satan's attacks, clearly defining that when a couple is not being sexual, this lack of self-control can lead to temptation and sin.

This is not a cop out to sin, but why wouldn't we take from this verse that God expects sex to be a very normal thing within all marriages?

Friends, if you don't take sex back from what it is in the culture and make it what God has intended for it to be, are your marriages being lived one hundred percent?

I like the idea that my spouse and I should be having the best sex in the world because we are Christians; my body is hers and hers is mine.

On the other hand, if I am obsessive, self-focused, or have all kinds of images in my mind from the past, how am I going to filter all of this into our godly and healthy marriage?

Let's talk about where the rubber meets the road. The reality is when a couple gets married, these two people are bringing into their marriage different perspectives, all kinds of experiences and expectations. What is the right amount of sex per, week, month, or day (LOL)? How far is too far and what is allowed? What stories have you heard or experienced that you have projected into being part of your marriage?

I remember a three-week series on sex and marriage where at the end of the series we answered the crowd's questions. "Can I dress my wife up as a prostitute" was asked? Within the answer it was made clear. Is the goal in this because you like prostitutes, because you like a certain kind of outfit, because you are living out some kind of past fantasy, or because you simply want your wife to wear something different in the bedroom?

The joke to this was, what if a husband was asked to dress up like a pirate; would it be because your wife had a thing for Johnny Depp?

God gave you one spouse as your standard for beauty, and she is the same spouse on whom to stir up this kind of love and be sexual with.

For you two now moving forward, how far is too far? What is allowed? And what should you watch out for? Have there been past hurts, abuse, situations you need to open up about, bring to the Lord, trust in Him that from here on out you can move on in the blessing of sex that He gives?

The author of Hebrews gives us a guideline to protect how our stories may play out:

Let marriage be held in honor among all, and let the marriage bed be undefiled, for God will judge the sexually immoral and adulterous.

Hebrews 13:4, ESV

We need to come to the marriage bed and honor ourselves, our spouses, and most importantly, God. Our being physical is most satisfying when we hear one another and understand how having a good sex life benefits us both.

For men, as much as women, sex begins with our interactions with one another and the words we say. Song of Solomon directs us to think of one another, speak affirmation and love over one another, which brings us to a place of trust and safety. Men, if we simply view our spouse's body as just a body, we are defaulting to the world's idea of sex. She is special; she belongs to God and to you. Be thankful and show her you are thankful.

Sex also needs to be something we approach humbly. How does your spouse's body work, what do they enjoy, what feels comfortable or even uncomfortable? Get away from the world's ideas that there is some kind of sexual standard, and throw away all the expectations you have ever had. Take turns serving one another and be passionate about the time you have set apart together. Part of your faith is learning how to enjoy one another.

There are going to be things one of you is more open to than the other. This means praying through and balancing out what works for both of you. Remember, Paul said that your body is your spouses, but this is also in itself mutual submission. I personally would encourage you to try different things, even if you don't think it may be fun for you, focus on serving your spouse, which in turn should be fun for you.

Obviously pornography, other people, or fantasies about other people are off limits and sinful. These things can lead to deeper and deeper sins and are all sexually immoral. Remember, the marriage bed should be "undefiled."

Also couples have all sorts of questions about foreplay, positions, and even toys.

I view sex between a couple just as Paul's view, that "your body," not just parts of it, is your spouses. That would mean you are free to explore, discover, and enjoy. Just be sure to set boundaries for things that may be shameful or abusive.

As far as people wanting to use toys and bring in all sorts of ideas, that I would leave between you and your spouse. But I will say that this body God has given you is perfectly enough for you to enjoy a fully sexually satisfying life. I personally do not see the need for such things and think it can lead to having to add more and more things to your sex life.

As a warning to you both, I would also challenge you on the topic of masturbation. I know this is being very blunt, but I remember attending a men's group where this topic was being discussed. One man's response was that this was something he did while traveling while thinking of his wife. Another man responded, "It was not your wife though." The point being made is that it was not his wife, but an idea in his head. Soon, this idea can become a place of lust where different ideas enter the mind, enter the relationship, and disrupt the balance. The men agreed that they didn't want to give space for anything to enter their minds in moments of weakness, and that being on the same page sexually as their spouse was best.

We have to acknowledge that sex is about sharing yourself with your spouse, about intimacy. Masturbation can separate yourself from that connection, and you may begin finding your own place of sexual satisfaction, one that doesn't depend upon unity with your spouse, to appease your own sexual appetite. If I can satisfy myself whenever I feel like it rather than depending upon my wife and our walk being intimate and godly, then before long, I will have my own little sexual world apart from my wife. This is not God's plan.

Believe me, I could have written an entire book on this whole sex topic, but for you as a couple today, do you need to spend some time talking through and praying through things, maybe even being sexual tonight? Give as much effort as you do to celebrate a birthday or an event to purposely pursue one another, not just romantically, but physically and sexually.

Will this lead to notes, texts, emails, more nights alone together, purposeful trips just to get away? For what suits your marriage, it should. This is love; don't be deceived.

Be blessed as you give your love life to God. And as we read this final verse from Song of Solomon, consider as we see the couple enjoy one another in marriage here who it is that ends the verse, who's aware of what they're doing, in the marriage chamber with them, encouraging them to enjoy this kind of love.

I came to my garden, my sister, my bride, I gathered my myrrh with my spice, I ate my honeycomb with my honey, I drank my wine with my milk. Eat, friends, drink, and be drunk with love!

Song of Solomon 5:1, ESV

DAY 27: A FAMILY AFFAIR

It is 8:30 a.m. right now, and I am waking up for the day. My wife is going to the hospital with her dad who is recovering from a heart attack and being treated. The kids will be up any minute, and as the day begins, I am aware that today, we as a family are putting forth the effort to go even deeper in our faith. Sure, Jude is only four, Eden seven, and Dakota fourteen, but Tracy and I both know, as we grow deeper and deeper in our walks, we see just how weak our flesh really is and how we need to make plans for the things of God.

Things like our family's path, our church attendance, Bible reading, and how we serve—we need to remind and encourage one another that life is constantly changing, and within each season, we need to keep our focus on Jesus and what we are being led to do.

Who knows how many more years are left for Dakota at home? I left for America when I was fifteen, and he is only a year away from that age. Eden is seven and seems more motivated by seashells than seeing everyone come to faith. And Jude, who is just four, sometimes looks more interested in the food he is playing with on his plate than who blessed us with it. Nonetheless, by God's leading, as the head of the home and with Tracy beside me, we know just how important our being purposeful in our family's walk together will be in our everyday lives.

In the Bible we hear so much about King David, but before he was a king, he was just David, a shepherd boy out in the fields honoring his father and tending to the flock. Was it not how he was raised that helped to shape his character and focus? Was his father Jesse not purposeful in the way he raised both David and his older brothers, walking with the God of their forefathers?

Could we not say the same for Daniel who "purposed in his heart that he would not defile himself" (Daniel 1:8, NKJV) while taken as a slave to Babylon?

Surely his parents understood the prophet Jeremiah's words as he spoke of the nation's coming exile, seventy years in total, but they went ahead nonetheless, having Daniel and raising him intentionally and with the mindset that God knew what He was doing and that He would want to use their son, even as God uses all of us.

What we are doing today is laying a foundation for our future. Despite everything you may be going or have gone through that brought you to this book, just as I have faced many things, we all need to push ahead, tweaking things as best we can to continue in the foundational things of the faith. As part of a family now, whether your own or even as part of God's family, how are you going to plan the things God has put in place for your family's growth?

Most of us know JFK's great statement from his inaugural address: "Ask not what your country can do for you—ask what you can do for your country" (January 20, 1961). This should be my mindset every morning, as I view my family as my country, my responsibility, and the sheep God has entrusted to me.

So as I begin to plan, will my wife be on the same page with me all the way to the end, as agreed last night? As you both look forward for your future, are you ready to be fully committed to task to get everyone to his or her destination safely? I know it is Jesus who is "the author and finisher of our faith" (Hebrews 12:2, NKJV), but we have to take hold of what is before us.

Am I mindful that as a teenager, Dakota's emotions are everywhere? He's soon becoming a man, and I am called to help shape him and provide him with a structure to help him through his Bible. I need to give him advice on books that relate to his age, how to be involved in the youth group, new friends, if it's time for him to start traveling the world with me, and wait for it, yes, even as he discovers girls. These next four years are going to be up there as some of the most important of his life; how am I taking that into account?

I could go on about Eden and Jude, about my wife's role alongside me, and how I will make room for where she feels God is leading her, and how we both need one another for this to be accomplished best.

What I am saying is that all too often I see a marriage, one that claims faith, where only one of the spouses really wants to take these things into consideration and contend for them. In many marriages, planning and structure is so foreign. Maybe this book has exposed holes in your relationship or even your Bible reading, and you are in danger of slipping back to square one, as if the pages of Scripture or even the time put into this devotional were just chaff in the wind.

Today is the day to consider your plans, your family's future, ways in which you can move things around and make sure you're intentional.

Here's a list of some questions. What might your answers reveal?

For example:

- Where are you as a couple going to attend church?
- Are you going to the same church together?
- Is there a midweek service that would benefit you to attend?
- What time are you setting apart for yourself to pray and taste of God's Word?
- Do you set time apart as a couple, to pray, read, and plan?
- How are you structuring Bible reading, prayer, and planning for your children?
- Where has God called you to serve, not religiously but sacrificially?
- What ways can you bring your children alongside you to see Jesus expressed?
- How do you guys structure your money, and is it stewarded over and used with God in mind?
- How can you as a family be missional, directly involved in the lives of unbelievers and shining the light of the Gospel both in word and deed?

Though these may seem like random questions, I can guarantee that within this simple list, something has stood out that you know would benefit your family and help sow into your overall future.

Each of these questions is significant because these are all things I see at work in the lives of maturing believers—by this I mean those who are pursing the things God has placed around them to help them mature. You would have a hard time missing it and falling back into old habits if your goal is to finish well.

My wife just left and the kids are all awake. Dakota is reading his Bible, Jude is asking for ice cream, which is not happening at nine in the morning, and Eden's about to get sucked into one of her handheld video games if I don't rescue her.

With all of this is mind, I purposely made this chapter shorter. Today, it would make sense to take some time to talk about and plan what matters to you both as you move forward as a family. What things do you know God has called you into to lead you and protect you? Where do you want to see your family in three months, six months, a year?

For me, I am going to gather the kids up, get out the Bible, read a passage, and invite the kids to talk about it. After this, we will talk about what or whom we can pray for. Mom should be home soon after and before the kids start homeschool, we can eat and spend time together. If today was overwhelming for her, we can put homeschool on hold and go for a bike ride or walk to change her focus.

So our days are structured in ways where, with what time we have, we put our focus on God, on one another, and then outward as we continue on this path toward maturity.

As the parents, it is your role your children will most follow and understand. You are the ones who get to pray, read with, bless, and help direct them as they grow. You are the ones who are able to be idle and get distracted by things that won't help structure the family.

I understand that some of this sounds challenging, but practically speaking, start with some small things, like biblical discussion or helping with one another's chores. As you do, patterns will be established, and as God directs, there will be more and more maturity as your family becomes more grounded in Christ.

DAY 28: MONEY! MONEY! MONEY!

Think about this: when Jesus, the Savior of the world and God incarnate, stepped into time two thousand years ago, He spent a great deal of His interactions with people talking about money and how people use or abuse it. His sandals walked the shores of Galilee and beyond sharing how eternity matters. But He also spoke a lot about money and how our understanding of it can reveal what is in our hearts.

As we head into the last few chapters of this book, where would we be if we avoided money within our marriages? Money is a part of every marriage, and how we view it, believe it or not, will dramatically affect our future.

Money was never really an issue for me and Tracy. Since I was a teenager, my skateboard career had provided more than enough to live on. It enabled us to buy a home, take care of our bills, and live comfortably. The fact that we were not extravagant, buying flashy and wasteful things, helped. The only time we really lost money was if we made mistakes or bad purchases, which is expected as you live and learn. This was all before coming to faith, having two more children, becoming a pastor in Huntington Beach, and traveling the world.

As that season shifted and my focus on skating changed, we were no longer living on a six-figure income from sponsors, royalties, and contests. No, we were dependent on the Lord. As our lives were being redirected, we would have to trust Him for how we should live, what our lifestyle would be, and ultimately what we should be content with.

Paul tells Timothy, "godliness with contentment is great gain" (1 Timothy 6:6). So as we were being led into a deeper relationship with Christ, God was beginning to address our hearts and the things we were depending on for satisfaction and comfort. This raises the question as to what kind of couple you may be and how you both view money, wealth, and the life God may have before you.

If as we entered this new season, my wife suddenly wanted the typical So Cal lifestyle, with a beachfront house, fine dining, and new cars, I would have missed my call by trying to work longer hours to provide for the idol in her heart, thereby making her the idol in mine, and in turn, making money our god. We would have ultimately been living above God's purposes, thereby putting even more tension on our marriage than what we already felt by living in a sinful world. Even worse, by dividing on where we stand on money, as with many couples, we could have separated. Yes, money as a focus does destroy marriages.

Is this to say that "having" is bad? No, but it is to say that many people are discontent when there is a perceived lack compared to others. Many a relationship has failed because one of the spouses had expectations about a standard of living, or they bought the "American dream." And while God was beginning to shape them for a life of service, the flesh got the better of them and one of the spouses bailed or resented the current situation. Again, the verse did say, "godliness with contentment is great gain."

Are we content with what God provides, what He has allotted to us? How can I pastor, travel, and preach humility while my wife and I are focused on building a materialistic empire here? I am glad you asked because Paul goes on to encourage Timothy, saying "For we brought nothing into the world, and we can take nothing out of it. But if we have food and clothing, we will be content with that" (1 Timothy 6:7–8).

He writes to his son in the faith, "Don't be caught up, distracted, or eager for the things that will not be eternal. Instead, be content with food and clothing." Paul's encouragement is simply to say, there's a path before you and time given; so, for what it will take you to gain the riches of the world and what you will have to sacrifice to work toward having such things, that will be a whole other call in and of itself.

This forced Tracy and me to confront who our master was. We had to take what we had been comfortable with and bring it to God. Did we have goals of buying house after house, a new car every few years, and being able to vacation whenever we choose? Was our marriage and purpose just about decorating a world that is actually decaying? Was Jesus lying to our faces when He said, "Do not lay up for yourselves treasures on earth, where moth and rust destroy and where thieves break in and steal; but lay up for yourselves treasures in heaven, where neither moth nor rust destroys and where thieves do not break in and steal. For where your treasure is, there your heart will be also" (Matthew 6:19–21, NKJV)?

No lying here. Instead, He is saying it is all a heart issue. What we do with His money that He gives us to handle temporarily reveals what is inside of us. And if our heart is here, focused on earth and this kingdom rather than His kingdom and eternity, then we will sow into what is here, enjoy what is here, and be robbed of investing for an eternal inheritance in heaven.

Jesus emphasizes this point even more, saying, "No one can serve two masters. Either you will hate the one and love the other, or you will be devoted to the one and despise the other. You cannot serve both God and money" (Matthew 6:24).

Did you catch that? Did He say, "God and money"? I would have said, *You cannot serve God and Satan,* but here we get insight into another enemy. Though money itself is neutral, it can be just as distracting and destructive as the lies of Satan. And we can be a slave to its power and platform.

To put this into perspective, as a couple is married, they have dreams and goals, will end up living in a home, purchasing cars, and planning for the future. Herein lies the issue with money. Who makes the decisions, who decides where it goes, how do you budget, and what will you do with your money?

Consider this: as money is squandered or misused, if a couple is not on the same page about finances and their understanding of how to use them, the marriage will fall prey to the weight and stress of debt, bills, or even worse.

For us personally, you may wonder how long it took for us to understand the pressure and concern pertaining to our bills, assets, and home after giving up my pro-skater salary. How often was the thought of providing for my family lingering before all other thoughts as I went about my day? It was constantly in my mind; daily I woke thinking of bills, family, and future. But as God was changing our focus from magazines, skateboards, product, and addressing our lack of understanding about money, He was also tightening the reins. We had to deal with how little effort we put out in regard to being good stewards over now, after becoming believers, what He provided and how to budget.

I say this to help you understand that generally there is a spouse who is responsible, is able to look ahead to the reality of rainy days and prepare for what may lay ahead. But if the other is a compulsive buyer, with no control over emotional shopping, you may wear your spouse into the ground and put tremendous strain on your future, even while saying you have faith and trust God to provide.

You can *trust* God all day, but if you are not a good steward over what He is providing for you to budget, then you will still feel the burden.

I like the saying: "if you birth it, you will have to feed it." In a nutshell, whatever you are giving birth to, the "have to haves" in your life, you will have to keep feeding them monthly, becoming enslaved to interest rates, credit cards, and loans.

Only recently, a couple heading into their later years in life made the decision to sell their home to get into a newer one with lots of improvements and in a more expensive area of town. They have a solid family, a good mortgage, and a casual life, with the freedom to serve in many places; they are available to do mission work and give lots of time to the community, yet they made this decision.

You can see the benefits from a worldly point of view. But from a heavenly perspective, they are now all the more enslaved to this brick-and-mortar location at such-and-such an address with such-and-such square footage.

They now have less freedom, have to work longer hours, are unable to eat out and visit with friends as much, and they will have to feed the tighter budget they gave birth to. So, was this really the best choice?

As American consumerism takes over, people are buying the lie that they must have that new thing to make them happy. We, as Christians, need to expose our hearts and desires and train ourselves to be content, especially within our marriages.

Within the last few years, my uncle passed, leaving his home to be split between my father and sisters. We were blessed to hear about some of the inheritance we would be getting. As it came in, it helped to take care of some out-of-place finances and provided more of a cushion in certain areas. During this time, I thought, *Man, if only this much money could come in every month!* But within a second after having this thought, I felt an impression instantly in my spirit: if God did begin to provide this much every month, how much more would I be accountable to budget and use this increase for kingdom work?

Yes, I would budget to provide a modest lifestyle for my family, but the question is: what am I storing up money here for? Shouldn't I be using it for eternal purposes?

Maybe you are a trust fund child or an owner of a successful business. Maybe you have plenty of money and never have to think twice about finances, except when it comes to charity and writing your check to put in the offering. Even then, we have to be careful; if we are giving with the wrong motive, it too can become religious. Simply stated, that once a week or month I put ink to paper or slide the card can actually just be a routine as opposed to an act of worship and service.

If you fall into this category, God has an even greater plan for your money than what you are currently aware of. Paul told us to "Command those who are rich in this present world not to be arrogant nor to put their hope in wealth, which is so uncertain, but to put their hope in God, who richly provides us with everything for our enjoyment. Command them to do good, to be rich in good deeds, and to be generous and willing to share. In this way they will lay up treasure for themselves as a firm foundation for the coming age, so that they may take hold of the life that is truly life" (1 Timothy 6:17–19).

He tells us not to put our "hope in wealth which is uncertain," but reminds us that God provides a life that sustains us "for our enjoyment." I take this to mean that as we live here, we should be able make our way through life living on what the Lord provides with the purpose of being "rich in good deeds … generous and willing to share." So our budgeting and planning should not be to outdo others: having the newest, always striving to be at the forefront. Instead, we should be using our resources and finances, along with our family plan and agenda, for the sake of others, in a life of servanthood. "In this way they will lay up treasure for themselves … for the coming age." If we live like this, then we will "take hold of the life that is truly life."

While this sounds so challenging for many to hear, this is based on the well-known verse just a few sentences earlier, which tells us: "the love of money is a root of all kinds of evil. Some people, eager for money, have wandered from the faith and pierced themselves with many griefs" (1 Timothy 6:10).

In your marriage, money is not what is evil. It is the desire for things, control, power, even a life of being content in myself and my ways as opposed to God's.

It should be clear by now, twenty-eight chapters into this book, that we are to filter and view everything through the Great Commission. So as my wife and I, along with our family, live out our calls to follow Jesus, He has the responsibility to provide for our "needs," so much so that He even encourages us not to be anxious about food, drink, or clothing.

"Therefore do not be anxious, saying, 'What shall we eat?' or 'What shall we drink?' or 'What shall we wear?' For the Gentiles seek after all these things, and your heavenly Father knows that you need them all. But seek first the kingdom of God and his righteousness, and all these things will be added to you."

Matthew 6:31–33, ESV

We should not worry or be concerned about the basic things needed to live because until God needs us to say goodbye to life here, He is obligated to provide those basics for us. In this verse, Jesus parallels the opposite of being content with what we have by pointing to the "Gentiles" who seek after "all these things," focusing more on their styles, how full their stomachs are, and if everything is up to their standard of living. God says that He sees what we need and will provide what we need, but we are to "seek first the kingdom of God and his righteousness, and all these things will be added."

Am I really content to seek first God's kingdom? Do I trust Him to provide for my needs but not necessarily my "wants"? How would life look for us if we didn't have everything we wanted but only what we needed? Would it do my kids any harm to learn to be content? Would it be a different witness of our contentment despite what prosperity preaching says?

Let's be clear heading into our marriages: Satan's goal is to have you reaching for more and more, never truly being content. But Jesus tells us to be content with Him and His call. Satan offered Jesus the world's glory in Matthew 4, but Jesus, knowing He only needed what His Father had set aside for Him and that His inheritance was literally "out of this world," knew where to focus and what to keep His life free from.

Keep your life free from love of money, and be content with what you have, for he has said, "I will never leave you nor forsake you."

Hebrews 13:5, ESV

We can have all we need today by putting God and His kingdom first. And while working hard at what He has given us to do, we can expect Him to add more as He sees fit for His purposes and for our enjoyment. If we don't have this mindset, that He knows what is best, it will be impossible to be content and our ever-evolving idols will direct our days.

He who loves money will not be satisfied with money, nor he who loves wealth with his income; this also is vanity.

Ecclesiastes 5:10, ESV

Are you satisfied? Does how much wealth you have now or how much you will have affect your marriage? Do we say no but still hear the flesh loud and clear shouting out for the satisfaction of this world? We need to address these very motives. Consider these questions from the book of James:

> What causes fights and quarrels among you? Don't they come from your desires that battle within you? You desire but do not have, so you kill. You covet but you cannot get what you want, so you quarrel and fight. You do not have because you do not ask God. When you ask, you do not receive, because you ask with wrong motives, that you may spend what you get on your pleasures.
>
> *James 4:1–3*

What are we fighting and quarreling about? What desires are causing this? We don't have what we want, so we become ruthless with one another, tearing one another to bits. We don't have these things because we are not asking, so hey, let's ask God! That sounds like a holy thing to do. But even in our asking, God is not going to give us what we are coveting because our goal in getting either the money to be able to purchase such things, or even in getting that which we desire is based on our own motives.

Don't get me wrong; I am not trying to mess with your head. But God's Word is clear in laying the foundation for your marriage pertaining to material things, money, and wants.

Since becoming a Christian eleven years ago and being called to full-time ministry, a lot has changed for our family of five. Before becoming a Christian, one of my last big purchases was a 2003 BMW 330i, a necessary buy for write-off purposes. That car is paid off now and I rarely use it as it challenges me. Is this false humility? As a guy raising support, how can I drive around in such a car, even if it is paid off, runs well, and has barely any miles on it? Pulling up to church events, what is the message it sends as I enter the parking lot? Would I buy a bigger version, maybe a more expensive car if I could? Is the Bentley the next goal if I could just justify it? Do cars have me? What is my home like? Do I store it all up and want more? Though I could say this is no one else's business, as a Christian, it really is everyone's business. I bought that car because it was reliable and a write-off, but today, what are my motives? I'm not here to judge anyone, but do we see the dangers attached to the kind of living that says Jesus is here to entertain all of my material desires?

It's our personal conviction that as our cars, home, clothes, and other things wear down, in faith, we will be provided with exactly what God sees as our needs in that season. As we step into those seasons, in prayer and looking up, the place of money within our marriages will be an essential representation of whether or not our hearts are on Him.

Believe me, those of the "name it and claim it camp" will not like this passage, but it is to you I say this: While you are storing up millions in things that shine, homes with rooms that are never used, and spent on things that proclaim power, it is actually God's money that is being stored up instead of being given for the sake of the kingdom. Instead, get the Gospel out, support those who need it, and use it for its actual purpose.

Tonight would be a good time to pray and consider the financial goals for your future. What tops the list of thoughts as you think about money? Is your hand closed or open? Would you invest more in things that are perishing than in lives being changed for eternity? Do you see just how missional money is? Are you a good enough steward to be able to use your income as a blessing to others?

My goal is not to micromanage your life, but to steer you out of danger and remind you to "Honor the LORD with your wealth" (Proverbs 3:9).

Believe it or not, biblically speaking, where our heart points in reference to our finances is a spiritual guide to where we are headed in our walks—good or bad. Finances, then, and how we use them should not be a burden, but simply a tool God uses to provide for us and that we in turn can use to provide and serve others.

DAY 29: IF ALL ELSE FAILS ... PRAY?

What did you do in that situation? How did you work it all out? What was it that you did to try and make sense of it all? You went to the doctor, got a diagnosis, started eating better, even got the right medication; what now?

Whether it's health, where to go to school, who to marry, where to attend church, what our call is, how often do we actually pray before we step into these things?

Where in the Bible, if I can be so blunt, do we see prayer as a last resort? Yet, how true to our lives this often is.

I understand that I am not Jesus, that I don't rise at the break of dawn every day, on my knees pursuing God with the most holy of prayers, or that every night, after all the chaos of the day, I don't always "withdraw" to pray and seek God's will. But is this not an example of how life will be best lived? To daily pursue God's plan and will for our lives, with this marriage and union included wholeheartedly?

Prayer should not be a backup plan, but the launching point into the path God has set before us.

By definition and as seen in Scripture, prayer is a time of pursuing, beseeching, petitioning, thanking, inquiring, praising, and ultimately, communicating with God.

So with as many books as you can read, sermons you can hear, with as much Scripture you can memorize and quote, is any of this actually going to change your life if you don't actually drench your days in prayer? The answer is a definite "no," not only because of the prayer itself but also because taking time to pray, sacrificing your time, is truly the expression of believing in those prayers. If not, why pray?

As I consider the mighty men of God who set their course and finished well, how often we see that it was prayer that clothed every step they took.

E. M. Bounds, in *Purpose in Prayer*, proclaimed, "Prayers are deathless," and how true and profound a statement. Grandmother's prayers are still being answered today decades after they were prayed and little old grandma has gone on to be with Jesus. Prayers of parents or family members over the lives of young ones are woven into the fabric of a child's days. Jesus Himself prayed, "Father, forgive them, for they do not know what they are doing" (Luke 23:34); and are not His prayers still being answered? He prays life into the dead men we once were and this prayer is applied to the salvation of every sinner who was without hope.

The best example of prayer in marriage would be Jesus Himself. "Jesus was married"? Yes, in a manner of speaking; He is going to be, to His bride—the church. The Bible itself is the story of a king going to war for His marriage, is it not? We see a picture of a spouse waging war by submitting to what's right for the benefit of the other, his bride, lost in another world.

With this idea in mind, we see Jesus—the Husband—petitioning God, aligning Himself with the marriage plan, clothing it in prayer even before events unfold.

No better place to see this than as He was preparing to go to the cross for us, His bride.

> Then Jesus went with his disciples to a place called Gethsemane, and he said to them, "Sit here while I go over there and pray." He took Peter and the two sons of Zebedee along with him, and he began to be sorrowful and troubled. Then he said to them, "My soul is overwhelmed with sorrow to the point of death. Stay here and keep watch with me." Going a little farther, he fell with his face to the ground and prayed, "My Father, if it is possible, may this cup be taken from me. Yet not as I will, but as you will."
>
> *Matthew 26:36–39*

Amazing that Jesus, the Son of God, aware of what He would be doing, even withdrew to pray and intercede for Himself.

As you and your spouse continue in this journey, just as we learned in the first ten chapters, God has a specific path for us. We have our own crosses that we need to own. And the reality is that this walk is one of prayer, pursing harmony with God daily. Jesus lets His emotions out as He gets before the Father and is "sorrowful and troubled." We see the human side of Jesus taking on the reality of this world, a husband taking on the day and its necessities for His bride, the church. As amazing as this picture is, seeing God in the flesh falling to His face, interceding for us, it is important that we recognize He is first and foremost praying for Himself to be in sync with His Father. If you as a spouse do not pray daily, in preparation for this race, for God's leading and His strength, you will depend more on the flesh than on the Holy Spirit.

> Then he returned to his disciples and found them sleeping. "Couldn't you men keep watch with me for one hour?" he asked Peter. "Watch and pray so that you will not fall into temptation. The spirit is willing, but the flesh is weak." He went away a second time and prayed, "My Father, if it is not possible for this cup to be taken away unless I drink it, may your will be done."
>
> *Matthew 26:40–42*

We see again Jesus praying and interceding a second time for Himself and for God's will to be done. He tells us that "the flesh is weak," and no perfect a time to say so than while even Jesus' own disciples "couldn't ... keep watch ... for one hour," their flesh failing through lack of spiritual discipline.

Since becoming a believer and walking the various seasons of marriage, I have seen time and time again that in seasons of chaos, attacks of the enemy, when all hell is trying to break lose, as I sit to gather my thoughts, how suddenly it comes to me that I have not been interceding in prayer for my marriage, for our family, for direction, and most importantly, for God's plan.

I am eager to jump through hoops, read all the marriage books I can get, post Scriptures all over the house as notes on the refrigerator, and through email; but to actually stop and pray can be difficult.

At this moment I remind myself that "the spirit is willing" and that though I am exhausted, out of options, and about to pass out alongside Peter in the garden, the reality is that the spirit is eager and ready.

When I choose to do this, not depending on my earthly methods, not trying to move the mountain myself, I am going to hear God all the more. This means for us as a couple that we will be awake, pursuing God, and able to do what Jesus called us to do: "watch and pray."

> When he came back, he again found them sleeping, because their eyes were heavy. So he left them and went away once more and prayed the third time, saying the same thing.
>
> *Matthew 26:43–44*

How both loving and convicting is this passage? In it, we see Jesus, who was given His own call to walk in for the love of others (His bride), going to war three times, giving to God His struggles, and affirming His call. What if Jesus would not have watched, what if He had fallen asleep and not depended upon the Spirit?

Prayer was not something Jesus just did in a random time of conflict, because now He was all the closer to being crucified. He didn't just finally understand how devastating it was going to be. No, prayer was always the biggest part of Jesus' day.

Very early in the morning, while it was still dark, Jesus got up, left the house and went off to a solitary place, where he prayed.

Mark 1:35

One of those days Jesus went out to a mountainside to pray, and spent the night praying to God.

Luke 6:12

He prayed before meals, before miracles, when there were battles, when there were victories, demonstrating for us what it means to "pray without ceasing" (1 Thessalonians 5:17, NKJV).

As I head into my sixteenth year of marriage, I am all the more aware that prayer will be the foundation upon which my days will hinge, whether I will represent God or not.

I'm the type of person who likes structure and who knows God is a God of order. And we see that Jesus gives us a pattern of thought and lifestyle in prayer in Matthew 6. He is not saying that we repeat these same words repetitively, as we so often see with prayer; but instead, consider the rhythms of thought if we really take this prayer before God and interact with Him, expecting His presence and direction daily.

"This, then, is how you should pray: 'Our Father in heaven, hallowed be your name, your kingdom come, your will be done, on earth as it is in heaven. Give us today our daily bread. And forgive us our debts, as we also have forgiven our debtors. And lead us not into temptation, but deliver us from the evil one.' For if you forgive other people when they sin against you, your heavenly Father will also forgive you. But if you do not forgive others their sins, your Father will not forgive your sins."

Matthew 6:9–15

I believe this prayer has in many ways become a treasure lost. Before I was even a Christian, I was repeating this in school, praying it before bedtime, hearing it said all throughout my childhood. But to stop and understand what Jesus is saying is mind-blowing. Consider as a spouse going before the Lord in the early morning and stepping into this posture of prayer.

"Our Father in heaven." Can you make a more serious statement? We've been redeemed, we are His, and we get to go to Him every day with all our issues, struggles, and shortcomings. And do you understand the volume of what it means for you and me to have this privilege? John tells us, "Now we know that God does not hear sinners; but if anyone is a worshiper of God and does His will, He hears him" (John 9:31, NKJV). Of course God can hear everyone else's prayers, but He doesn't respond to them, not until there is a cry of repentance and a true turning to Him, despite what everyone believes.

When I wake in the morning, aware that God Almighty hears my prayers, it makes those moments all the more special. And not just God the title, but Jesus even says Father, *Abba*. To put this nowhere close to what it means but still make the effort, it's as if you and I had been in trouble with the law but had access to the judge, one who was not only willing but eager to listen to us and show us favor. Yes, this is how radical of a posture Jesus is encouraging us to approach God with.

"Hallowed be your name." As we sit in the posture of conversation and connecting with our Father, we also are putting everything in life in its right place, as I like to say, consecrating it unto Him. Hallowed is a Greek verb *hagiazō* that means to cleanse internally, to purify, to dedicate to God.

Everything: our walk, families, our jobs, how we treat people, our boss, sex, money. It's in these moments of prayer that we are reminded of something: as much as God cares about His children, there is one thing far above that expression of love, that being His name lifted up above all else. If not, we are missing it.

"Your kingdom come." This mindset declares that God's kingdom is not of this world; we are only aliens here temporarily, but God's kingdom is within all Christians (Luke 17:21). Therefore, our mission daily is to shine the light of God's kingdom. As we pray with these things in mind, our focus will begin to turn to how we are living and what we should be doing.

"Your will be done, on earth as it is in heaven." Your will? What is the Lord's will? For me to win every skate contest, for people to serve me, a raise, be my own boss? Though God can do whatever He wants in my life, through this prayer, Jesus shows us that God's will manifested in my life is the greatest of purposes and it should not be a burden, but a privilege.

"Give us today our daily bread." As simple as it sounds, when we awoke one day and asked God to do as He has intended in our lives, we are positioning ourselves to receive from Him whatever He chooses. This was my posture when my mother passed and my wife miscarried, and things held together. It's through the good and the bad that I have to be able to say, give me this day my daily bread, all that you may. And I'm fine with it. Are you?

By now we have spent some quality time with God, have opened ourselves up, have lined up our day to receive. But before we head out, "forgive us our debts, as we also have forgiven our debtors." Ouch! Yes, this is a place to bring your struggles, the sins that are crouching, or the doors you may be stepping into that are not of God. Here, early in the day, is where you can come to God for strength and also bring to mind things that may have happened to you, something someone did that was sinful toward you that you too might now need to forgive and forget.

As we are ready to live out this day, as so often is missed, we are even to pray that God would "lead us not into temptation, but deliver us from the evil one." Lead me away from myself, from my struggles, from the things that I have within my sin nature: my anger, lust, control, bitterness, or the rest I may carry, even praying that I would be delivered from Satan's attacks. He is not saying those attacks will prosper, pertaining to salvation and our future, but we should be aware of his schemes alongside our current weaknesses. After all, he did not hold the fruit up to Adam's and Eve's mouths, did he?

To wrap up my times of prayer, for myself, my wife, family, friends, even enemies, I sometime have prayer lists, verses, requests, or sometimes nothing. Sometimes just asking God to lead in the Spirit what needs to be prayed about or brought to mind.

We are not to repeat this prayer because the wording is powerful. But this posture and pattern of bringing everything before God, realizing we can do nothing without Him, that He has given us the Holy Spirit to help us daily on mission, to confess our sins, forgive others, and resist the enemy, helps us to live a faith-filled life. This leads us to declare: "Yours is the kingdom and the power and the glory forever. Amen" (Matthew 6:13, NKJV).

My suggestions here are that you would find your patterns and rhythms of prayer with God. Sometimes in the morning, sometimes in the night, sometimes both … that you would know one another inside out, considering family, children, friends, and enemies. That you would develop definitive times of prayer both alone and also together, while being still before the Lord, but also daily while life is coming at you, always listening and pressing in to what God is leading you to.

Tonight would be a great night to open up for deeper and more pursuant prayer, even basing it around the key verses we looked at:

"In this manner, therefore, pray: Our Father in heaven, hallowed be Your name. Your kingdom come. Your will be done on earth as it is in heaven. Give us this day our daily bread. And forgive us our debts, as we forgive our debtors. And do not lead us into temptation, but deliver us from the evil one. For Yours is the kingdom and the power and the glory forever. Amen. For if you forgive men their trespasses, your heavenly Father will also forgive you."

Matthew 6:9–14, NKJV

DAY 30: GO, BE THE BRIDE!

So here we are; time to say goodbye ... the end of a thirty-day focus on marriage. Time to focus on the next thing, or not?

If this is simply the end of a book for you, then the greatest accomplishment here may be finishing this chapter.

But by now, with us hopefully exposing ourselves all the more and digging deep into our foundations, establishing what truth we stand upon, today, by all means, should actually be the beginning.

This is not simply the ending of a book, but an invitation to become a leading role in the story of your life and marriage.

These past eleven years as a Christian, I have always been amazed at how many people are afraid to venture into the book of Revelation, even though it begins by telling us "blessed is the one who reads aloud the words of this prophecy" (Revelation 1:3). This end-times book reveals to us a vision given to John from Jesus—about His church, about events that will unfold, about God's judgment, but also about the only story we can truly say ends with a "happily ever after."

Revelation is a book that reveals some of the darkest times in human history, much like the struggles we may go through in marriage.

It reveals times of strain and struggle, misunderstandings and victory, but it ultimately ends on the reality that the LOVE of Jesus Christ, the very Word of God, never fails. He whom this book is based upon and by whom we are currently being led forth, His love NEVER fails. Our marriages must be sustained by this truth.

We are given the end-times' picture that plays out before God's throne, one that consummates in heaven and restores that which was lost in the garden.

This event, which will be the most significant in all of human history, is the one in which Jesus Christ Himself is married to the bride He died for, the church.

"Hallelujah! For the Lord our God the Almighty reigns. Let us rejoice and exult and give him the glory, for the marriage of the Lamb has come, and his Bride has made herself ready."

Revelation 19:6–7 ESV

After every word spoken, human interaction, verse shared, message preached, Bible read, witness slain, cheek slapped, night of prayer, move of the Spirit, life taken advantage of, hardened heart, regenerated soul, it is all worthwhile because at the end of time, we hear these words: "Hallelujah! For the Lord our God the Almighty reigns. Let us rejoice and exult and give him the glory, for the marriage of the Lamb has come."

The end of time, when it is all said and done, Jesus Christ Himself will be spending eternity with His bride, you and I who are in Christ for all eternity, the picture of love, dedication, commitment, sacrifice, and marriage.

When we read the book of Revelation and consider its ending, we have to come to our senses. No matter what is happening around the world—who the president is, what is happening with Israel, how my life looks, how situations are playing out, the folly I have fallen into, or the blessing I may have received—the goal and purpose for every person in Christ, married or not, is to live his or her days representing their upcoming marriage to Him. Yes, it is that profound yet simple.

We need to close out this book encouraged and eager.

Even as I finish this, I am aware that my own marriage is to be a representation of Christ, and Tracy and I both desire to grow more into Christ's image. But we sometimes need to ask some tough questions.

Do I walk as though my wife and I left our fathers and mothers to be united as one? Do I lay down my life for her, loving her as Christ loved the church? Does she, as we both submit to the Lord, submit to my headship as I try to steer this ship with her by my side? Are we in tune with God by prayer and growing in His Word. Are we living on mission for those around us? Is the Holy Spirit Himself the leading voice as I seek to be led and empowered to do all of this? Have I forgiven my spouse and others, aware that offenses will come and sin is crouching? Am I eager to live this life interacting with those of the faith, knowing we all have our own personal gifts and talents that should be used to encourage one another as we step into the living waters of our faith? Am I aware that all of this is the story of God Himself at work in the lives of His people reaching the lost by shining the truth?

Paul best summed this up in his letter to the church in Ephesus, pointing to how two become one, even as we are now hidden in Christ and covered by His blood: "This mystery is profound, and I am saying that it refers to Christ and the church" (Ephesians 5:32, ESV).

It has been well over a year since starting this book. My phone and emails have been filled with more and more stories of broken homes, shortcomings, and also victories since that time.

I began by being moved to write this book because of a couple who had struggled with infidelity. What a great testimony to Jesus' power that today they are doing better than ever; they are closer, more unified, aware of their struggles, and deeply involved in family and purpose.

Yes, it can happen. Through Jesus!

Of all that my wife and I have shared with such struggling couples over this year, the foundational truths are those found in this book. I am not talking about the stories, though they give us a context for how things played out. But I am talking about the verses, the Scriptures, God's voice of promise into our lives. Knowing couples would have heard our story of restoration, perhaps through the "I Am Second" ministry or from Billy Graham's "My Hope America" video series, I hoped it would lead more people to ask about how we made it through, what keeps us going, and how they too can walk on established paths.

My hope and prayer is that as you, the reader, arrive at the end of this book that you would first and foremost have a great love and understanding for our Lord and Savior, Jesus Christ, and that this love would roll over into a life of seeing how God's Word leads and guides us as the Holy Spirit empowers us.

May you truly "seek first the kingdom" from here on out.

As I sit here on the couch next to my beautiful wife, Tracy, this Saturday morning waiting for our three children to awake, know I am praying for the readers of this book—for your marriages, separations, shortcomings, and future.

I would ask that you would please pray for my marriage, that we would continue turning to the Lord in all we do and represent His voice to the world through this beautiful interaction of marriage that God orchestrated and is sustaining.

Who would have known that those words spoken over us all those years ago would become the hope our lives are built around? We who had snuck off to Vegas, amidst the worldly love, dead in sin, and far from God, can point back and see His faithfulness in our marriage. And not just our marriage here and now, but our eternity, that when God sent His Son into the world to die for it, what we actually see expressed and accomplished is:

"LOVE NEVER FAILS."

BRIANSUMNER

"How can they **hear** without someone **preaching** to them? And how can anyone preach unless they are **sent?**" Romans 10:14-15

Since coming to faith in 2004, Brian's platform as professional skateboarder opened doors for him to begin to travel, sharing the story of redemption from the pages of Scripture and from his own life, his marriage, and his family. Today, Brian is a volunteer pastor at his local church. He spends the rest of his time both in his local community and traveling the world: sharing at outreaches, churches, schools, recovery centers, conferences, on mission wherever God leads. This is possible because in 2014, his home church encouraged him to step out in faith and trust God to raise support to travel, even as the apostle Paul did.

If you would like to personally partner with Brian and stay up to date with the ministry he is doing, please visit: **www.briansumner.net/support**